# THE JAPANESE LANGUAGE IN
# CONTEMPORARY JAPAN

# AEI-Hoover
# policy studies

The studies in this series are issued jointly
by the American Enterprise Institute
for Public Policy Research and the Hoover
Institution on War, Revolution and Peace.
They are designed to focus on
policy problems of current and future interest,
to set forth the factors underlying
these problems and to evaluate
courses of action available to policy makers.
The views expressed in these studies
are those of the authors and do not necessarily
reflect the views of the staff, officers
or members of the governing boards of
AEI or the Hoover Institution.

# THE JAPANESE LANGUAGE IN CONTEMPORARY JAPAN

Some sociolinguistic observations

Roy Andrew Miller

901.71

American Enterprise Institute for Public Policy Research
Washington, D. C.

Hoover Institution on War, Revolution and Peace
Stanford University, Stanford, California

AEI-Hoover Policy Studies 22

**Library of Congress Cataloging in Publication Data**

Miller, Roy Andrew.
    The Japanese language in contemporary Japan.

    (AEI-Hoover policy studies; 22) (Hoover Institution studies; 58)
    Bibliography: p.
    1.   Japanese language—Social aspects.   I.   Title.
II.   Series.   III.   Series: Hoover Institution studies; 58.
PL524.M5        495.6        77-5661
ISBN 0-8447-3247-8

*Printed in the United States of America*

# Contents

INTRODUCTION .............................. 1

## 1 THE MYSTICAL FRAMEWORK ................. 9

Watanabe's Characterization of the Japanese Language 9
James's Marks of the Mystical Experience 14
James's Marks and Sociolinguistic Themes 16
Origin of the Japanese Language 19
Loanwords in the Yamato Vocabulary 25

## 2 THE ESSENTIAL DIFFICULTY OF THE
LANGUAGE .............................. 29

Kindaichi's Testimony 30
Newspaper Accounts 32
Suzuki's Testimony 35

## 3 INADEQUACIES OF THE LANGUAGE ............ 41

Suggestions to Replace Japanese 41
Japanese as Imperfect and Impractical 45
Suggestions to Adopt Japanese 51

## 4 THE WRITING SYSTEM ....................... 53

Enduring Authority 54
Experience of Understanding 57

**5** A MODERN THREAT TO THE ANCIENT
LANGUAGE ................................ 61

    Ono's Approach to the History of Japanese  62
    The West as Corrupter of Japanese  65

**6** IDENTIFICATION OF THE RACE AND THE
LANGUAGE ................................ 71

    Linguistic Homogeneity  73

**7** REACTIONS TO FOREIGNERS' SPEAKING THE
LANGUAGE ................................ 77

    The Law of Inverse Returns  78
    Suzuki's Documentation of the Law  79
    Suzuki's Analysis  82

**8** CONCLUSIONS: THE NEED FOR CAUTION ....... 91

    Central Role of the Myth  92
    Lack of Demythologizers  94
    Antiquity and Durability of the Myth  95
    Derivative Myths  97
    Translation and Interpretation  98

BIBLIOGRAPHY ............................. 103

# Introduction

Japan has grown steadily in importance for the United States since contacts between the two nations began in the mid-nineteenth century. Today Japan is a preeminent industrial power integrated into the Western world politically and economically, and the ways of life in both countries have much in common. Americans can identify with intensely urban Tokyo or marvel at Osaka's burgeoning industrial complex. The many surface similarities, however, can obscure the different cultural legacies and disparate cultural values that underlie the two societies. The actions and activities of the members of any society are inevitably influenced by the extent to which the members have inherited their culture; actions reflect in varying but important degrees the members' participation in and understanding of their cultural heritage. Thus, it is imperative for anyone concerned with Japan to acquire some appreciation of the distinctive cultural patterns underlying Japanese society.

Like many important tasks, however, this is easier said than done. If any outsider is presented with a catalogue listing all the characteristics of a given culture, he will undoubtedly find within the list elements that appear to be mutually incompatible or nonsensical. These incongruities gradually disappear when the connections among the various parts are understood, but the task of perceiving these rarely articulated relationships is difficult.

One way to begin the challenging process of exploring a different culture and acquiring some feeling for the impact it has upon its mem-

Author's Note: I would like to acknowledge my gratitude to Larry Kahn of the American Enterprise Institute for his invaluable help in preparing this manuscript.

1

bers is to examine a discrete facet of that culture. Such an intentionally limited study has several advantages. First, this type of study is manageable because it focuses upon a small range of topics and does not require intimacy with every aspect of the culture. Second, connections among the various parts within the single facet studied may provide hints and clues to the overall patterning of the culture.

## Focus of This Study

In this study an attempt will be made to gain some insight into the inner workings of Japanese society by focusing on one facet of the culture: the Japanese language, as viewed and evaluated by the Japanese themselves. By examining the language in detail, some of the underlying principles that distinguish Japanese culture should also become visible. Studies by the Japanese about their own language and their comments about it appear to be a particularly fruitful component of the cultural matrix for examination because these writings superficially contain paradoxes, omissions, and errors that obviously do not puzzle the Japanese.

A related question that has troubled me for years and, in fact, provided the initial inspiration for this monograph is, Why do so many passages in Japanese texts of all periods, but particularly in the written language of modern scholarship and intellectual discourse, read perfectly well in the original but turn out to be so vapid when rendered in a fairly literal English translation? Within the field of linguistic scholarship this problem is particularly acute because little of what contemporary Japanese scholars write and publish in Japanese could be published intact in a literal English translation without becoming the butt of amazement and even ridicule abroad. Yet these works, which are widely read in Japan, are by eminent men writing in their own fields.

One partial answer to this paradox must be that in modern Japan the vocabulary and rhetoric—indeed, one is tempted to speak of the dialect—of almost all writing about the Japanese language and Japanese linguistics constitute an extremely specialized and highly sophisticated vehicle of communication, a virtual meta-language. It is a language in which the words when taken together, both in the context of the writing and in the overall context of the sociocultural background out of which they grow, end up meaning something different from what they appear to mean when taken one by one. But translation generally deals with

2

words on a one-by-one basis. This, of course, is true to some extent of all language, and it is why translation is always more or less unsatisfactory; but the situation seems to me to be particularly true of the language of scholarship that deals with Japanese language and Japanese linguistics.

Another answer lies, I am convinced, in the existence of a large body of assumptions concerning the nature of the language and the way it operates within Japanese society and culture. These assumptions, which are generally held by Japanese intellectuals, are most often unverbalized but nonetheless real, and as a body they approach the status of full-fledged folklore. Japanese intellectuals are familiar with the outlines, details, and ramifications of the body of assumptions, but most non-Japanese are not. I believe that there may be some value in bringing at least a portion of this generally held body of assumptions about the language out into the open and providing interested non-Japanese readers with the opportunity to acquaint themselves with it.

The area of contemporary Japanese sociolinguistic speculation has something else that recommends it to our study, namely, the surprising abundance of published materials available. A flood of books concerned with the language appears in Japan every year. Many of them sell very well, and the genre as a whole is of perennial popularity. This phenomenon is particularly clear-cut at the present time, when modern Japanese intellectual circles are being churned about at considerable velocity with questions of the so-called *Nihonjinron*—that is, questions of national identity: Who are we Japanese? Where did we come from? Where are we going? Sociolinguistic issues play a major part in such questions, and they deserve our attention for this reason, if for no other.

The non-Japanese reader will be surprised, if not incredulous, to learn of the amount of energy and effort in Japan that goes into writing and publishing books that deal exclusively with questions about the language. It is virtually impossible to go into a bookstore in any Japanese city and not find on the table nearest the entrance a great pile of new publications that deal exclusively with the questions treated in the present monograph: What *is* the Japanese language? Is it a good language or a bad one? Do we Japanese use it correctly? Does it use us Japanese correctly? And on, and on. The literature is vast, disparate, and of tremendously uneven scholarly level, ranging from the serious and the informative to the purely sensational.

The problem here has been to pick and choose among the many

3

available published sources, and the single greatest difficulty has been to decide what not to include in these pages. Still, despite its bulk, this sociolinguistic literature of modern Japan is almost unknown abroad. Foreign scholars have either scorned or overlooked it, and attempts by Japanese scholars to make it known in foreign languages have generally met with failure. The attempts in the present monograph to summarize some of its main themes and to render some of its more significant passages and expressions into English are the first comprehensive introduction for English-language readers to its scope, dimensions, and surprisingly rich content. The existence of this sociolinguistic literature is a key that provides us with access to an area that, because it is initially puzzling, should prove useful to explore in order to enlarge our perspective of Japanese culture.

The present monograph focuses on some of the special features of the rhetoric and on some of the assumptions that are basic to the thinking and the writing of many Japanese intellectuals when they consider the question of how the Japanese language operates in Japan today and in Japanese society and culture. In a word, it is concerned with sociolinguistics, and my hope is that it will provide a somewhat better understanding of some of the essential features of this important field. Obviously, the highly technical areas of linguistics proper are not the place to start, and I have avoided them in these pages as far as possible. When it has been absolutely necessary to become involved in the technical aspects of linguistics, I have tried to supply the reader with the necessary technical information in the simplest terms possible. This will probably strike the linguist as both oversimplified and unsatisfactory.

Rather than becoming involved in questions of linguistics proper, I have attempted to focus the discussion on the vast literature of contemporary Japanese sociolinguistic speculation. By this I mean the many books, monographs, and learned papers, including articles and letters in the daily press, that in one way or another deal with the working of the Japanese language vis-à-vis Japanese society and speculate about the problems that are caused by the daily operation of the language within Japan. Although this whole area bears only a tangential relationship to the field of linguistics proper, it does have the great advantage of providing a relatively simple means of access into the subject as a whole. It does not involve highly technical linguistic issues; rather it deals with problems and questions that are more or less familiar to persons in almost any modern culture, including our own.

4

## Structure of This Study

This monograph is divided into eight chapters. Each seeks to present data relating to one aspect of contemporary sociolinguistic thought in Japan, together with the necessary minimum of analytic framework that will allow the reader to put this data into a meaningful perspective. The chapters do not deal with totally disparate subjects, and there is some overlap in content among them. By and large, however, the data and analysis have been arranged according to the following scheme:

Chapter 1 proposes an overall analytic scheme into which most of the sociolinguistic data treated in this monograph appear to fit. Within this framework, the question of the genetic relationship of Japanese to other languages is briefly considered. The question is treated here not in its technical linguistic aspect but solely for its sociolinguistic importance.

Chapters 2 through 6 extend this analytic framework in detail, assembling evidence from a variety of sources and expanding the treatment suggested in Chapter 1. Chapter 2 is concerned with overt indications in the sociolinguistic literature of the society's concern for the *inexpressible* character of the language; Chapter 3 with the unexpected shifts in direction that occur when the language is, by way of contrast, *poor-mouthed* in that same literature; and Chapter 4 with evidence for the experience of *overwhelming understanding* and *enduring authority* conveyed by the language. In Chapter 5 this experience is shown to be essentially *transient*, despite its *perpetual afterglow*; in addition, consideration is given to the concept of the West as corrupter and polluter of the Japanese sociolinguistic experience. This latter theme leads directly into Chapter 6, in which contemporary sociolinguistic approaches are studied for their possible identification as continuations of the old concept of *national polity*, on several different levels, with particular concern here for problems involving linguistic monolithism and linguistic minorities in modern Japan.

Chapter 7 considers the problems that arise when Japanese comes into confrontation with foreign languages, especially the problems involved in the use of the Japanese language by foreigners. This chapter attempts to suggest some of the reasons that underlie the often surprisingly negative reaction that many Japanese have to the spectacle of non-Japanese employing the Japanese language with any degree of fluency.

After this survey of aspects of the language, we will be in a position to sketch a few general conclusions, identifying the principal themes
revealed by the investigation. As the title of this last chapter indicates,
these conclusions are best expressed as a series of *cautions* concerning
various aspects of the contemporary Japanese sociolinguistic situation,
particularly as it involves bi- and multi-lingualism and the problems of
translation.

What I have tried to do, within the area of my own professional
competence, which is primarily in the fields of linguistics and language
learning, is to survey the popular Japanese sociolinguistic literature in
order to see what it has to teach us, on the one hand, about the ways
in which the Japanese today approach their own language and, on the
other hand, about their approach to us when we become involved with
that language. This sociolinguistic literature is fascinating, and the
present monograph only scratches its surface. I have been particularly
interested in this literature ever since I first learned of its existence, because it seems to me that it provides an unusually unclouded view into
Japanese life and society. This view is all the more valuable because
most of the sources that I have employed here are written and published in Japan for Japanese readers under the tacit assumption that
foreigners will never see or read them. Thus, it has not only the charm
of the unknown but also the fascination of the forbidden.

Robert Shaplen, writing in a "Letter from Tokyo" in *The New
Yorker*, described the current flood of interest in questions of national
identity in Japan extremely well:

> The foreigner, or *gaijin*, himself an object of suspicion and
> constant, cautious scrutiny, quickly becomes aware that the
> Japanese are increasingly scrutinizing themselves in their own
> private way, scanning themselves as if through either end of
> one of their excellent telescopes, trying to decide, in the sort
> of cinematic or theatrical game they so enjoy playing, whether
> they look big or small.[1]

One of the things that the Japanese keep scanning in this way,
trying to decide whether it looks big or small, is the Japanese language.
The scrutiny goes on in the literature of sociolinguistics. This alone
should be sufficient to make this literature of value to the student of

---

[1] Robert Shaplen, "Letter from Tokyo," *The New Yorker*, vol. 50 (May 20, 1974),
p. 105.

modern Japan, quite apart from the fact that this literature deals directly with the most remarkable of all the identifiable constellations of Japanese social and cultural behavior patterns—the Japanese language.

## Restrictions in Scope

Several caveats are needed before the study is begun. The reader should be aware that I have made a conscious effort to avoid one segment of the sociolinguistic literature, namely, works by Japanese who have lived abroad, taught the Japanese language to foreigners while they were abroad, and later written about their experiences and their sociolinguistic speculations concerning the Japanese language and its role vis-à-vis Japanese society.[2] Admittedly this is an interesting subsection of the sociolinguistic literature and is deserving of study. Nevertheless, it seems to me that these authors approach their subject with too many specialized preconceptions and that they have, in the course of their generally long residences abroad, effectively negated their own value— for purposes of this study, at least—as informants on the topics I am addressing here. They already have, or think they have, the answers to the questions that I propose to study. I do not suggest that their answers are necessarily wrong, but I prefer to arrive at my own, by studying the responses and the data supplied by informants who are not writing for the sole, or even the main, purpose of answering the specific questions most of interest to me here.

I have tried to limit my use of published sources to works that are directed to the wider Japanese reading public and whose authors approach their subject matter simply in their capacity as Japanese intellectuals, without the special knowledge or the special advantages—or disadvantages—gained by long residence abroad and daily contacts with foreigners. These sources appear to me to be more reliable informants. But the reader of this monograph must constantly keep in mind that

---

2 This genre is represented by Ikeda Makayo, *Soto Kara mita Nihongo, Washinton daigaku no 'Nihongo Kurasu'* [Japanese seen from the outside: the University of Washington's Japanese language classes] Sanseidō shinsho [Sanseidō new library], no. 29. (Tokyo: Sanseidō, 1968); Ikeda Makayo, *Nihongo saihakken, ishitsu no ninshiki* [The rediscovery of Japanese: my realization of its different nature], Sanseidō shinsho, no. 117. (Tokyo: Sanseidō, 1973); Itasaka Gen, *Nihongo yokochō* [Back streets of the Japanese language] (Tokyo: Shibundō, 1975); Bernice Goldstein and Kyoko Tamura, *Japan and America: A Comparative Study in Language and Culture* (Tokyo: Charles E. Tuttle Co., 1975).

7

what is considered here from this enormous literature is only the tip of an iceberg. Of course, I hope that I have chosen the most significant portions of the literature, but selection involves subjective judgments whose accuracy cannot be guaranteed.

In addition to published sources, I have also made considerable use of information collected on a number of field trips in Japan during which I interviewed people of various backgrounds concerned with different aspects of questions about the Japanese language. Again, the problem has been what to include and what to leave out, and more has had to be left out than could be included. I believe that this evidence from interviews—although I have not attempted to document it in detail in these pages—fleshes out the data from published works in a way that is vitally necessary if the present study is to be more than a library exercise—if it is to approach closer than that term suggests to the realities of contemporary Japanese life.

Also, the restricted scope of this study dictated that not all influences affecting the language be considered. For example, I have made a conscious attempt to avoid questions of the economic aspects of sociolinguistic behavior in modern Japan, although I fully realize that any social science study that totally ignores the economic dimension is by that very fact less than complete. My excuse for this is lack of space and my own lack of competence in this area. Nevertheless, such economic questions are surely important. For example, in 1972 the *New York Times* quoted an executive of a New York-based company to the effect that it would cost the company between $40,000 and $50,000 to bring an American businessman out to Japan and keep him there for a single year, while for between $2,000 and $3,000 they could "teach the average Japanese to speak English well enough to take over the work of an American."[3] In view of the double-digit inflation since 1972, and even making all possible allowance for journalistic hyperbole, such statements make it clear that the economic considerations of sociolinguistic behavior in Japan—especially that segment of such behavior involving foreigners with the Japanese language—must also be studied. I regret that I have not been able to do it here.

---

[3] *New York Times*, May 28, 1972.

# 1

# The Mystical Framework

In 1974 Japanese consular offices in America began distributing to their "cultural and educational" mailing lists copies of *Japan Echo*, a glossy new public relations magazine. In the second issue of this English-language journal, an extremely important article by Watanabe Shōichi, entitled "On the Japanese Language," appeared.[1] This article, which had been published earlier in Japanese, supplies a framework for our entire discussion.

Watanabe possesses all the credentials necessary to serve, in this fashion, as a semi-official government spokesman for the orthodox viewpoint concerning the nature of the Japanese language and its relation to Japanese social behavior: he is a university professor, holds a doctorate in Western philosophy from a German university, and now specializes in teaching English literature in Japan.

### Watanabe's Characterization of the Japanese Language

In his article, Watanabe presents four characteristics of the Japanese language that, according to him, interact to give the language a unique character. First, he examines the *waka*, a traditional poetic form of thirty-one syllables. He argues that these poems typify the peculiar Japanese approach to their language because, through the rules governing their construction, these poems embody and preserve the *koto-dama* ("spirit of the language"), which he sees as the most important charac-

---

[1] Watanabe Shōichi, "On the Japanese Language," *Japan Echo*, vol. 1, no. 2 (Winter 1974), pp. 9-20.

teristic of the language. Watanabe acknowledges that this spirit of the language "is admittedly quite bizarre according to the modern way of thinking."[2] By studying the ancient *waka*, however, some of the features of *koto-dama* can be discerned: "[o]ur ancestors had a very special feeling toward *waka* . . . which, I am convinced, can provide a clue to what exactly was the 'spirit' of the Japanese language."[3]

An examination of the structure and language of these poems allows Watanabe to construct a thesis he calls "equality before *waka*." The thesis is based on the consideration that the *waka* do not use—or better, are not supposed to use—loanwords from Chinese or other foreign languages in their poetic diction.[4] Foreign loanwords, according to Watanabe's argument, presuppose the existence of an elite stratum within the society because only the educated would know these words. But an elite contradicts equality. Hence, all men are "equal before *waka*," with their purely Japanese diction from which all foreign elements have been rigidly excluded:

> This is a strange phenomenon. But what is stranger still is that no one has ever criticized the phenomenon as being strange. Be this as it may, it is thanks to such an intellectual climate that virtually all Japanese could participate in poetry composition, while women and children who knew nothing about the Chinese classics could allow themselves to freely comment on *waka* composed by Oe-no-Masafusa, an authority on Chinese classics.[5]

In the present context it is sufficient to note that Watanabe shows himself to be squarely in the mainstream of the Japanese sociolinguistic literature with his blatant mixing of literary considerations and genuinely linguistic factors. He shifts back and forth quite freely between these two spheres in his attempt to postulate a spirit of the language on the basis of rather less than complete descriptive statements concerning its literature.

Building upon this foundation of the dictates controlling poetic

---

[2] Ibid., p. 10.
[3] Ibid., p. 12.
[4] Here rules are apparently made to be broken. Prince Mikasa used the English word *belt-conveyer* in the poem that he contributed to the January 1965 ceremony that celebrates the beginning of a new year of court poetry (the event that is usually, though somewhat inaccurately, reported in the Western press as the "Emperor's Poetry Contest"). Details appear in Roy Andrew Miller, *The Japanese Language* (Chicago: University of Chicago Press, 1967), pp. 266-267.
[5] Watanabe, "Japanese Language," p. 15.

composition, Watanabe attempts to explain why the Old Japanese poetry recorded in the two earliest Japanese historical texts—the *Kojiki* (Records of ancient matters, 712) and the *Nihon Shoki* (Chronicles of Japan, 720)—is written in Old Japanese rather than in Chinese, as is almost all the rest of both works. He sees this fact following from, and at the same time documenting, the "profound sense of awe and respect toward the Japanese language" possessed by the authors of these texts, as well as their conviction that the ineffable contents of the Old Japanese poetic corpus could not and should not be translated into Chinese. In this way, he argues, "the two books manifest a clear-cut idea about the native tongue, which goes to the root of the Japanese identity."[6] Watanabe endorses the sagacity of these ancient scholars because "ancient Japanese poems generally lack logical elements, which therefore are unfit for translation to be made available for foreigners."[7] Like the ancient Japanese, he sees the Japanese language as containing an indescribable or ineffable quality.

That something indescribable or ineffable should be the identifying feature of a language might appear to be a significant methodological drawback. According to Watanabe, however, the ancient Japanese poems possessing *koto-dama* contain a second characteristic that complements their ineffable quality: "when read in the originals, these poems open to the reader a 'vista of an extensive area,' including numerous other ideas analogous to what they literally present. Thus, the reader will have his 'mental consciousness' invigorated and may even become carried away with emotion."[8] The Japanese language, as it is utilized in these poems, serves to expand the reader's mental horizons. This again occurs in an indescribable and nonquantifiable way; it is the quality of being noetic.

Watanabe here interrupts his discussion in order to consider an extremely pedestrian and literal English translation of an early Old Japanese poem.[9] In his view, the poem has a content of inner, mystical

---

6 Ibid., pp. 11-12.
7 Ibid., p. 15.
8 Ibid., pp. 15-16.
9 In a somewhat less wooden translation than appeared in the article, the poem in question reads as follows:
"Countless are the mountains in Yamato,/But perfect is the heavenly hill of Kagu;/ When I climb it and survey my realm,/Over the wide plain the smoke-wreaths rise and rise,/Over the wide lake the gulls are on the wing;/A beautiful land it is, the Land of Yamato!" Translation in Nippon Gakujutsu Shinkokai, *The Manyōshū*,

experience and meaning that certainly resists and indeed all but defies translation, that is, any communication of its true content and message to anyone but a Japanese. As he puts it, this is because:

> Seen rhetorically, or in terms of its superficial, semantic contents (which may be communicable to foreigners in translation), this unsophisticated poem is almost equal in quality to a scribble a middle school child on a school excursion might make on a postcard for home.[10]

These are harsh words indeed, particularly since they come from an avowed champion of the Japanese spirit and are being given worldwide distribution in English by the Japanese diplomatic establishment. We can here only note in passing that the concept that translation into English is a valid standard against which both the Japanese language itself and monuments of Japanese literature may somehow be measured is inherent in Watanabe's remarks.

From within these seeming weaknesses, however, Watanabe is able to extract strengths that further refine the elusive nature of the Japanese language. He contends that the vague, but nevertheless real, expansion of understanding that occurs when a Japanese encounters a specimen of the Japanese language, such as the Old Japanese poem that he discusses, is experienced only briefly, but that it is nevertheless felt permanently. The argument he presents is internally consistent, and it even approaches the elegant in its simple circularity. Though he concedes that the poem in question is literally puerile, at the same time he argues that it is this very element of puerility that in and of itself provides both a transient moment of revelation and a lingering afterglow. But it provides them only for a Japanese, who by the very fact that he is a Japanese is placed into a different relationship with this admittedly puerile poem because for him it is something that can open a "vista of an extensive area." What is dust and ashes in the mouth of the foreigner becomes the bread and wine of life itself for the Japanese:

> Nevertheless, this much [that is, reading the *Man'yōshū* poem in question in the original] is almost enough for Japanese to have their souls stirred. The only possible explanation is that in the emperor's poem, there is *koto-dama* at work, which is

---

*The Nippon Gakujutsu Shinkokai Translation of One Thousand Poems* (Tokyo: Iwanami Shoten, 1940; reprinted, New York: Columbia University Press, 1965), p. 3.
[10] Watanabe, "Japanese Language," p. 16.

warrantable among the Japanese people as a whole. It is neither a question of the transfer of logical ideas nor that of intellectual comprehension, but one which concerns something close to the "mental capacity for the formation of genius," as referred to by Kant. . . . Kant used the word "genius" as meaning the capacity of man to create a world of ideas which are logically unfathomable to a third party. Foreigners can hardly keep up with Japanese when the latter allow themselves to become carried away with emotion.[11]

Following this, Watanabe hints at a fourth characteristic of the Japanese language that again is due, according to him, to the special potency of the ancient language. For Watanabe, when *koto-dama* operates it is equivalent to a superior power whose effect is to lift up, indeed to seize and hold captive, the human soul during the whole course of the experience. This becomes even more evident in a subsequent passage from the same article, in which the discussion is directed toward identifying the repository of this superior power:

Yamato words, which are intertwined with *koto-dama* of ancient times, emerge in the mind of men when *something* pulls at their heartstrings, while borrowings from Chinese are employed at a time when the mind is intellectually at work for external development. In other words, in the realm of verse, the Yamato language is often the vehicle by which to describe the mind moving introversively and yearning for *something* to embrace, whereas borrowings tend to be indiscriminately used when the mind is extroversive, ambitious and aggressive.[12] (italics added)

By "Yamato words" Watanabe simply means words of Japanese origin, particularly in contrast to the later elaborate layers of Chinese loanwords that constitute most of the modern Japanese vocabulary.[13] It

---

[11] Ibid.

[12] Ibid., pp. 18-19.

[13] Studies of the proportion of Chinese loans to Yamato words in early literary texts have shown the rapidity with which borrowed lexical items found their way into the language, at least into the varieties of language reflected in written records: "the *Taketori monogatari* [The tale of the bamboo cutter] (early Heian period) has 90 Chinese words: a representative section of the *Makura no sōshi* [The pillow-book of Sei Shōnagon] (mid-Heian) approximately equal in length to the *Taketori monogatari* has 720 Chinese loanwords; and a similarly representative sampling of the *Konjaku monogatari* [Modern tales already old] (late Heian) has 1,498 Chinese words." Miller, *Japanese Language*, p. 245. In modern times, and particularly with the great increase in literacy brought about by compulsory education, this tendency has been tremendously accelerated.

would, of course, play havoc with Watanabe's thesis to attribute any ability in the direction of this mystical "grasping by a superior power" to elements of the Japanese lexicon that are transparently of foreign origin. How could words that everybody realizes have been imported from China be admitted to be capable of pulling at the Japanese heart-strings?

Watanabe thus presents four salient features of the Japanese language that he believes work together to shape its impact upon the Japanese. To put the disparate characteristics that he identified into a coherent framework, we will jump briefly from the East to the West and use an analysis supplied by the nineteenth-century American philosopher William James.

### James's Marks of the Mystical Experience

In *The Varieties of Religious Experience*, James elaborated upon a proposed fourfold categorization of "mysticism, its ecstasy and its experiences." This was part of his ground-breaking application of pragmatism and experimental psychology to the study of religious phenomena. In this scheme James attempted to isolate and identify four marks that, when observed to be present in a human religious phenomenon or experience, would justify our calling that phenomenon or experience *mystical*. James's four marks of mysticism were, in order of their importance, the characteristics of being ineffable, noetic, transient, and passive.[14]

It would be difficult to locate any ready-made analytic framework that would more precisely or more compactly supply a system of reference points along which we might proceed in a survey of contemporary Japanese views and opinions on the Japanese language, particularly a survey of contemporary Japanese approaches to the Japanese language as a sociolinguistic phenomenon involving relations with non-Japanese. The system that James proposed for categorizing and analyzing the in-

---

[14] William James, *The Varieties of Religious Experience: A Study in Human Nature* (New York: Macmillan Co., 1961), pp. 299-301. The passage concludes as follows: "These four characteristics are sufficient to mark out a group of states of consciousness peculiar enough to deserve a special name and to call for careful study. Let it then be called the mystical group."

ternal structuring of the phenomena of religious mysticism fits representative modern Japanese attitudes toward the Japanese language surprisingly well. This is immediately shown by the close similarities between James's categories and Watanabe's analysis. But also, James's rationale behind his concept of the mystical experience can help to integrate the baffling and often amorphous information about how the Japanese view their language.

Religion is not an important consideration in modern Japanese society, and indeed has not been a significant force in Japanese intellectual life for centuries. When religion was still important, Japanese religious life had more than its share of the truly mystical. Indeed, some of the world's most important varieties of the mystical as religious experience saw their finest flowering on Japanese soil, notably in the various Japanese versions of the Zen schools that had been brought over from Buddhist China. Today, when Zen is alive and well in Los Angeles but for all significant purposes dead in Japan, and when all other forms of religious expression are all but without impact or meaning in the daily life of the Japanese people, it is tempting to see in the views and opinions that are so widely held by modern Japanese concerning their own language the gradual evolution of a full-scale sociolinguistic surrogate for the religious experience itself—particularly of a surrogate for those very elements of mystical ecstasy that were so interesting to William James. Modern Japan may not really have lost a religion after all; it may instead simply have gained a language, to which its approach is essentially that of the mystical adept toward his own ecstatic experiences.

To appreciate more fully the surprising congruences between James's categorization of mysticism and the dominant views held by many representative Japanese intellectuals concerning the Japanese language, it is necessary first of all to see a little more of what James wrote about each of his four marks of mysticism.

The first mark, ineffable, is the quality of defying normal, rational, or common verbal expression. James found this mark "the handiest" one of the four, but he also noted that it is in a sense the most difficult. It is surely a negative mark because as soon as the subject has described this feature of his experience he immediately goes on to say that it simply defies further expression. The second, or noetic, mark is that of providing an overwhelming experience of understanding: "illuminations, revelations, full of significance and importance, all inarticulate though

15

they remain; and as a rule they carry with them a curious sense of authority for aftertime."[15]

James believed that these first two marks were in themselves sufficient evidence for classifying any state or experience as mystical, and that the last two, while usually found in conjunction with the two above, were as a rule less clearly defined. The third mark, transient, has to do with the fact that the states in question appear incapable of being sustained over any considerable period of time. The final mark, passive, refers to the state in which the subject describes himself as somehow "grasped" by some superior power. With "mystical states . . . some memory of their content always remains, and a profound sense of their importance. They modify the inner life of the subject between the times of their recurrence. . . ."[16]

### James's Marks and Sociolinguistic Themes

James's four marks of the mystical experience dovetail closely into the major themes of almost all the available literature by Japanese about the Japanese language in Japan. The mark of ineffable finds expression in the Japanese literature about the language along two major courses of development. One course has to do with the difficulty of the Japanese language—its difficulty, we must note, for Japanese as well as for foreigners. The other course concerns the difficulty, if not the impossibility, of translating characteristic modes of Japanese linguistic expression into foreign languages, particularly (but by no means exclusively) the problems of translating traditional Japanese literature into English.

A subordinate theme related to this supposed difficulty of the Japanese language for the Japanese themselves is to be found in the frequently expressed concern for the ambiguity of the language. Again, this is largely a matter of concern in the use of Japanese by Japanese, though the theme also is encountered frequently in discussions of problems of translation.

The noetic mark follows in close step upon the ineffable mark in the Japanese views of Japanese, just as it does in James's original formulation of mysticism. Even though the "subjects" are unable to give any coherent account of what has been happening, they agree that their

---

[15] Ibid., p. 300.
[16] Ibid., p. 301.

experience of understanding has been overwhelming. In the case of the Japanese language, this noetic mark finds its most direct expression in statements to the effect that the language somehow has an overwhelming significance and a profoundly moving content for its speakers and users, notwithstanding the earlier admitted impossibility of presenting any description of the dimensions of that significance and content. From this mark also follow the tremendous importance that contemporary Japanese society places upon the language and the tremendous amount of time and energy that are devoted to writing and thinking about it. Since the experience of understanding that the language involves is vast, overwhelming, and without limits, it is only proper that the concern and effort expended upon the language by the society should in turn be as extensive, as well as intensive, as possible. The response is in just proportion to the stimulus. This noetic facet of the contemporary Japanese sociolinguistic experience also probably helps to explain the facility with which the society continues to accept, indeed at times even appears to relish, the tremendous waste of energy and labor involved in the perpetuation of the cumbersome modern Japanese writing system, despite its multiple collisions with the demands of modern technology and high-speed telecommunications.

Just as predicted in James's formulation, the last two marks of mysticism are somewhat less clearly visible in Japanese sociolinguistic thinking and writing. But their presence can be detected. The sociolinguistic complement of James's mark of transient is probably to be identified along two different, but intersecting, paths. The first path involves an important segment of the traditional literature—namely, the tiny formal constructions of individual Japanese poems, the seventeen-syllable *haiku* or the thirty-one-syllable *waka*. The physical limits of these miniature verse forms are themselves the ultimate structural and formal metaphors, as it were, for that transiency of human affairs that is more often than not also the principal theme of their literal content.[17]

---

[17] This is neither to imply nor to suggest that the principal structural feature of Japanese poetic forms has always, or consistently throughout the history of Japanese literature, reflected brevity. In the early periods in particular, Japanese poetic forms were distinguished by the lengthy integrated sequence, in effect producing poems of great length and poetic structures of considerable magnitude. For an introduction to the study of these early forms of Japanese poetic composition, see Roy Andrew Miller, *'The Footprints of the Buddha,' an Eighth-century Old Japanese Poetic Sequence*, American Oriental Series, vol. 58 (New Haven: American Oriental Society, 1975). But these earlier, extensive poetic structures

But like the transiency of the mystical experience, the transiency of the *haiku* or *waka* is apparently accompanied by an afterglow that may very well last a lifetime, as claimed by Watanabe.

The second path that indicates the existence of a transient quality in the language also involves these ancient verse forms. Many Japanese writers in the field of the sociolinguistic approach to Japanese specialize in recapturing during later periods of tranquility the essentially transient, but supremely important, moment of elation. This moment of breakthrough illumination is well expressed in a *haiku* or a *waka* because its momentary, transient, once-in-a-lifetime quality finds in these short verse forms the most precise formal analogue possible. If such a specialist believes that the general population is not being provided with the full opportunity for free access to the rewards of such experiences, transient though they may be, he may devote a considerable amount of effort in attempting to remedy this defect.

If the transient mark is the most subtle of the four to identify in contemporary Japanese sociolinguistic behavior, the fourth is, by contrast, almost too clearly in evidence. The evidence of the materials available clearly points toward the conclusion that the modern Japanese tends to feel himself completely passive as he rests in the grip of his own inherited language. This grip provides support and comfort, but at the same time it may be identified as a restraining force and even at times as a barrier between the subject and the outside world. Possession by outside spiritual forces works in two different ways. What is a reassuring force of outside momentum, lifting the subject up and out of himself, when viewed in one fashion, can also be an almost unconquerable pressure that tends to retain its passive subject in its powerful grasp forever.

The modern Japanese inherits his language. His membership in the group of speakers of the language is as automatic and passive as his membership in his race. The identification of these two memberships with one another, along with their common and essential passivity, is an important facet in the modern patterning of Japanese sociolinguistic behavior. The single most important consequence of these two interlocking automatic memberships is that questions of language and its

---

were soon abandoned and so completely forgotten that their very existence had to be "rediscovered" by modern literary scholarship. In the meantime, the tiny formal constructions have provided the dominant structural theme for all Japanese poetic expression.

usage in contemporary Japan almost instantly become racial rather than linguistic questions. From this there follow in turn several other important, if equally unexpected, correlations that have to do with the learning and the use of Japanese by foreigners.

This fourth mark of passivity also helps to explain the surprisingly complex constellation of self-doubts and internal questionings that distinguishes almost all contemporary Japanese discussions of the learning of foreign languages by the Japanese themselves. Learning a foreign language inevitably involves changing one's own language for another, if only for intervals of a few seconds. This necessity, which is inherent in all language-learning situations, immediately comes into sharp confrontation with the culture's passive acceptance of its own language as a necessary and inevitable portion of the very fact of being Japanese by race and birth. The entire range of the specter of alienation—alienation from the social fabric, alienation from the nation, alienation from the race itself—immediately becomes involved in even the simplest foreign-language situation in Japan. This goes far to explain the tremendous difficulties that most Japanese so readily admit to facing in the course of learning any foreign language. It also helps to explain why genuine opportunities to learn a foreign language are so rarely provided by the Japanese educational establishment—that is, opportunities for gaining practical, working control of a given foreign language, as distinct from solving the intricate grammatical puzzles that still constitute the bulk of the foreign-language portions of all university entrance examinations. This is not surprising once we view it in the framework of the present formulation. The Japanese educational system is the principal guardian of the nation's social fabric. It would be expecting the extremely unlikely if we were to suppose that the educational system could combine this essential role as a national guardian with the simultaneous role as a destroyer of that same fabric. Given the nature of the Japanese sociolinguistic situation, it would be precisely such destruction of the social fabric that the education system would have to undertake were it ever to facilitate genuine learning of a foreign language.

### Origin of the Japanese Language

It is only within the framework of the Japanese language as a mystical experience that many otherwise initially inexplicable positions concerning the language begin to make sense. A striking example of this is the

19

contention that Yamato words—theoretically, words of pure Japanese origin—form a pure foundation for the language and possess special qualities that give the language a mystical nature. As we have seen, these words are central to Watanabe's argument that the language has a unique influence over the Japanese.

On the face of it, Watanabe's analysis, which is analogous to many others, appears to be based upon a fairly rigorous attitude of historical linguistics. When we consider the matter more deeply, however, we are forced to conclude that any attempt to make a hard-and-fast dichotomy between Yamato words and foreign loanwords in Japanese of any historical period, but particularly in modern Japanese, breaks down almost immediately. Watanabe argues that the Yamato vocabulary can be clearly established and that by simple definition it consists of nonforeign, nonimported lexical elements. By the very fact of their historical origin, these linguistic elements are totally free from all taint of foreign origin. He further concludes that this Yamato vocabulary is operative as the linguistic embodiment of that "superior power" by means of which the *koto-dama* of the Japanese language lifts up and takes over the psyches and intellects of its passive speakers. Unfortunately, the situation is not that simple. Indeed, almost none of these conclusions can be made to square with established linguistic data, not to mention the general theory of historical linguistics.

No language comes from nowhere. Historical linguistics can show where languages came from and where the discrete elements, including their vocabulary, came from. It does this by describing in more or less detailed fashion something of their earlier stages and then by establishing the changes and steps necessary to account for the observed differences between these earlier stages and the attested forms of historical times.[18] Such study does not prove that one language is related to another, but it can in many instances assemble increasingly convincing evidence that points in that direction. The proposed dichotomy between Yamato forms and loans into Japanese is real enough, when and if it can be established by historical linguistics. But Watanabe, as well as other scholars who work along similar lines, has manipulated the dichotomy so that it tends to become almost solely a mystical factor and not at all a criterion of historical linguistics.

---

[18] For an introduction to this rather technical question, see Miller, *Japanese Language*, chapter 5.

Here for the first time in these pages we encounter the use of an overtly routine scientific concept or term from Western linguistics for essentially nonlinguistic ends. In this case, the distinction between loanwords and inherited lexical stock is used in the attempt to document the mystical *koto-dama* of the Japanese language. Although he uses scientific terminology, Watanabe does not conduct the discussion along modern, scientific linguistic lines.

Where did the Japanese language come from, and where did the Yamato words originate? Only one of two hypotheses is possible regarding the ultimate origin of the Japanese race and the Japanese language. One hypothesis is that both the people in question and the language they now speak were uniquely evolved (spontaneously generated, as it were) in the same Japanese islands in which they now live, and hence they have no connection, historical or genetic, with superficially similar human beings and superficially resemblant varieties of human speech to be found elsewhere in the world. This seems more than a little unlikely and, indeed, it may be all but ruled out on geological grounds alone. The geological evidence for the age of the Japanese islands simply does not provide sufficient time to accommodate the long process that would be involved in a totally independent evolution of human beings and human speech solely within the confines of the Japanese island chain and totally without either massive borrowings or massive inheritances from other stocks, both ethnic and linguistic.

Yet it is this unlikely assumption of a totally independent evolution of mankind in the Japanese islands that underlies the speculations of Watanabe and his many colleagues when they attempt to correlate spiritual, mystical, and racial considerations with the historical origins of the Yamato elements of the Japanese vocabulary. Such attempts are doomed from their onset since they are based on this implausible assumption concerning the origins of Japan and the Japanese. Independent evolution of man in the Japanese archipelago is possible—insofar as anything is possible. But it is so extremely improbable that it must be ruled out of serious consideration. It can be an acceptable explanation only to those who propose that the Japanese language is a unique system of mystical experiences rather than one of the world's many linguistic systems.

The only other possible hypothesis is that the Japanese are somehow genetically related to some other human stock (even though opinions may well differ as to what that stock was). Those who opt for this

21

assumption must necessarily break with Watanabe's approach through mysticism and ecstasy since they are committed to the existence of some genetic link between Japanese and some other language or languages in the world. The language (or languages) may still exist or it may be lost to history, or at least lost to written records, but it nevertheless was simply another variety of human language. The link may be hard to establish and difficult to document, but that does not prove it never existed.

Although they are in the minority and generally do not occupy important professorships in the national university system, there are Japanese scholars who have chosen to disassociate themselves from the first position sketched above. They are divided among themselves concerning just where in the world one should look for the evidence of such links. Basically, they are divided into three camps: those who argue for a genetic relationship between Japanese and the Altaic family of languages, those who favor a genetic relationship with the Malayo-Polynesian family, and those who see Japanese as a mixed language that somehow contains elements of both the Altaic and the Malayo-Polynesian groups. The present study is not the place to consider the scholarly arguments for or against any of these positions.[19] The important point for our purposes is simply the fact that there are scholars who acknowledge the genetic relationship of Japanese to other languages and who are trying to establish such a relationship by the normal methodology of linguistics.

Within this context, the concept of a special spiritual or mystical role in the culture for "pure elements" of the Yamato vocabulary simply cannot be maintained historically or linguistically. The Yamato words—like the Chinese loanwords and like everything else in the language—must eventually have come from somewhere else. In language, as in life, nothing comes from nothing. The Yamato words do not, because historically they cannot, in any way represent or correlate with any *koto-dama* that is distinctively Japanese, or unique, or ineffable and mystical.

Several of the major figures in Japanese language study in Japan, and even several major Japanese scholars in the field of historical linguistics, have taken the nihilistic position in their work that "the genetic

---

[19] For a full discussion of these matters see Roy Andrew Miller, *Japanese and the Other Altaic Languages* (Chicago: University of Chicago Press, 1971).

relationship of the Japanese language can never be established." This is particularly true of the group of scholars known as the Tokyo school.

The usual Japanese linguistic terminology for the genetic relationship of one language to another reflects the negative approach of the Tokyo school. Japanese linguistic scholarship has dichotomized its terminology relating to the problem into two watertight compartments— one for Japan, the other for the remainder of mankind.[20] The term *shin'en kankei* and its synonym *shinzoku kankei*, both literally meaning "genetic relationship," are in general usage by scholars in Japan, particularly by members of the Tokyo school, for all languages other than Japanese. But for Japanese, and for Japanese alone, the term is *keitō*, literally "lineage" or "inheritance." The never-ending, and by definition never-to-be-solved, study of the problem of the genetic relationship of Japanese to other languages is always called *keitōron*, "the problem of the *keitō*," referring to Japanese and to no other language. A leading Japanese authority on questions of language and linguistics has even defined the terms *keitō* and *keitōron* in this fashion in a standard dictionary of Japanese linguistic terminology. He writes that the terms *shin'en* and *shinzoku kankei* are used in Japanese scholarly writing when linguistic relationships are, or can be, known, as typically in the case of foreign (that is, European) languages; but *keitō* and *keitōron* are used when these relationships are not, or cannot be, understood, as in the case of Japanese.[21]

For the scholar of linguistics who is outside the structure of Japanese society and culture and who is familiar only with the Western methods of scientific inquiry concerning the possible genetic relationships of languages with one another, it will certainly be surprising to find that the most important school of Japanese historical linguistics actually takes as the point of departure for its studies the a priori conclusion that nothing will ever be discovered in the course of those studies that will in any way contribute to the solution of the question they are investigating.

---

[20] For a sociolinguistic treatment of several aspects of this tendency toward an ingroup versus outgroup dichotomy in the Japanese language, see Roy Andrew Miller, "Levels of Speech (*keigo*) and the Japanese Linguistic Response to Modernization," in *Tradition and Modernization in Japanese Culture*, ed. Donald H. Shively (Princeton: Princeton University Press, 1971), pp. 601-667.

[21] Roy Andrew Miller, "The Origins of Japanese," *Monumenta Nipponica*, vol. 12, no. 1 (1974), p. 94, nn. 1 and 2.

But no single element in any reasonably complex culture makes sense to the outsider until he manages to view it within the larger context of that culture itself, or until he succeeds in surveying it in terms of the internal relationships that exist between the various structural members of that culture. The scholars of the Tokyo school of Japanese historical linguistics—who so stoutly maintain that it is now, and will continue forever to be, impossible to establish any convincing data concerning the genetic relationship of the Japanese language to other languages in the world—are working along lines of inquiry that are perfectly consistent within their own sociolinguistic culture. Indeed, these lines of inquiry are virtually interconnected with the principal structural elements of that culture, no matter how much the approach of this school may appear to the outside observer to depart from the accepted norms of scholarly investigation. The nihilistic, a priori point of departure for members of this school is their own mystical experience of and in their own language. Everything in their scholarship hinges upon this. Like all other mystical ecstasies, this experience is ineffable, and this ineffability is then advanced, in their thinking, to the status of a position-defining dogma.

For these scholars, Japanese is not simply a language but an ineffable sociolinguistic experience. Although this experience is incapable of explanation to the outsider, it remains meaningful beyond description to the members of the group. Membership in this group, however, is available only by the accident of birth. To all others, the experience of the language must remain meaningless folly. What is unique in this fashion can obviously only have had a unique origin; this in turn directly and effectively rules out any possibility of demonstrating a genetic relationship between Japanese and any other language or languages anywhere in the world. No myth anywhere in the world has ever been able to tolerate simple, mundane births for its heroes and god-kings. So also, simple, genetic inheritance from some other linguistic stock must a priori be ruled out of consideration if Japanese is to preserve its unique, ineffable character and play its full role in the sociolinguistic myth. Thus, what might at first glance appear to be a system of inquiry flying directly in the face of both reason and logic, not to mention scientific method, proves to display internal consistency and, indeed, an elegant economy of argumentation when viewed as a constituent part of the cultural structuring out of which it has itself grown.

# Loanwords in the Yamato Vocabulary

Quite apart from the historical questions of the genetic relationship of Japanese to other languages, Watanabe's approach to his subject through the concept of the "Yamato words . . . intertwined with *koto-dama* of ancient times . . . that emerge in the mind of men when something pulls at their heartstrings" will not hold water on the purely descriptive level. Regardless of where the Japanese language as a whole came from—that is, regardless of its eventual genetic relationship to other languages—there is abundant evidence that even the very earliest layers of Yamato words are shot through with loanwords from other languages. Early loans from Chinese and Korean are clearly evident, and loans from many other languages probably exist, though they are not as easy to document.[22]

No single element in the Yamato vocabulary is more redolent of the ineffable, heartstring-tugging *koto-dama* than the well-known word *ume* ("flowering plum"). How often the ancient Japanese poets, and for that matter Japanese poets of all periods, have used this vital lexical item in their work of moving the minds of men to deep emotion and mystical ecstasy! But the word *ume* (Old Japanese *umë*) is a loanword into Old Japanese from Old Chinese, just as surely as the plant to which it refers is one of the many introduced to the Japanese islands from the continent shortly before the historical period. Thus, linguistic science can only conclude that the Yamato vocabulary operates quite as well in its work of "pulling at the heartstrings" with borrowed as with native lexical materials. For when the Japanese poets were singing of the *ume*, they were singing about a foreign tree, and they were referring to it with a foreign term, that is, with a Chinese loanword, albeit one of considerable antiquity within their own lexical stock. The borrowed merchandise seems to operate within the system quite as well as the native product—if, indeed, any of the latter can be identified.

But many important Japanese language scholars approach the question of the existence of loanwords from the initial position that such loans simply could not have taken place. This approach from the basis of negative assumptions fits in quite well with the equally nihilistic approach of most of the scholarship about the relationship of Japanese to other languages. The established position of this approach was under-

---

[22] Examples in Miller, *Japanese Language*, p. 170.

25

scored by the distinguished Japanese linguist Hattori Shirō, who until recently held the most important post in Japanese historical and comparative linguistics in the entire national university system. In the preface to the 1957 printing of his collected essays on various aspects of the *keitōron* question he wrote: "[If by publishing the present collection] I am able to demonstrate that the genetic relationship of Japanese is not a question that can be solved by many years of research, I shall have achieved one of my goals."[23]

This negative approach makes sense only within the overall context of the contemporary Japanese sociolinguistic attitude toward the nature and history of the Japanese language. It can be followed in all its involved meanderings only when we understand how central to that sociolinguistic approach is the concept of the existence of a pure Yamato level within the Japanese vocabulary—a level totally uncontaminated by any loan materials whatsoever. Such a concept, however, simply cannot be maintained in the light of what is generally known about the origin of the Japanese language.

At this point, the scholars of the *keitōron* question, with their strident insistence upon the total insolvability of the question of the genetic relationship of the Japanese language, join forces with scholars who insist upon the impossibility of early Chinese loans ever having entered Japanese. Both have had to assume their chosen roles because of their deep involvement in the mystique of the Japanese language as an experience of ecstasy. Torn from that context, their views are difficult to understand, much less to support. But viewed within the overall analytic structure proposed in the present study, in which the Japanese language becomes a modern mystical experience central to the concerns of the society as a whole, they display perfect external, as well as internal, consistency.

Watanabe's article has done us a great service, for it has provided us with the initial evidence supporting a framework upon which we may now base our further and more detailed consideration of the questions that here interest us. Watanabe's editors probably do him less than full justice in their cryptic introduction to his paper, in which they pay him the following rather backhanded compliment: "The readers of this article will realize how difficult it is to translate Japanese into other

---

[23] Hattori Shirō, *Nihongo no keitō* [The genetic relationships of the Japanese language] (Tokyo: Iwanami Shoten, 1957), p. iv. Author's translation.

26

languages." They are too modest. The reader of Watanabe's article will find in it an almost perfect structural microcosm of those main themes in terms of which the modern Japanese scholar most often approaches all these questions. And of course, the fact that the Japanese diplomatic establishment felt that the article was important enough to be included in the second issue of its *Japan Echo* should also not be overlooked. By providing this prominent and elaborate forum for Watanabe's discussion of the Japanese language, they document in the most effective manner possible just how seriously contemporary Japanese society takes all the sociolinguistic issues under discussion here. With Watanabe's contribution in hand, we are now in a good position to examine in greater detail other aspects of the contemporary Japanese sociolinguistic approaches to the Japanese language. But in the course of what follows we will uncover little that is not already hinted at in Watanabe's treatment or that does not find comfortable accommodation under one or another of William James's four "marks of mysticism, its ecstasy and its experiences."

# 2
# The Essential Difficulty
# of the Language

The first mystic hallmark of the Japanese language—its being essentially and by definition ineffable—finds its most overt expression in the contemporary sociolinguistic literature in the form of references to the difficulty (*muzukashisa*) of the language. That the language is difficult for foreigners goes without saying, but much is also made of the fact that it is difficult for the Japanese themselves. This point is made over and over again in modern publications on all possible levels aimed at a wide variety of Japanese reading tastes and talents. The passages that may be cited from the literature in this connection leave no doubt that it is the Japanese language itself and not simply its complex writing system to which the authors have reference.

Of course, no language is truly difficult for its native speakers. Every native speaker in a natural sociolinguistic entity who does not suffer from some mental or physical handicap has achieved complete control over his or her own language by the early teens, and the question of difficulty does not enter into the picture. These comments about difficulty so frequently encountered in the contemporary Japanese sociolinguistic literature can be understood only within the overall analytical framework of the Japanese language viewed as a mystical experience of ecstasy, closely parallel to religious experiences of mysticism in other cultures. When they are understood in this fashion, they easily fit into the overall structuring of the sociolinguistic approach of the culture. Otherwise, and particularly to the linguist operating without reference to the structuring of Japanese culture and society, they are meaningless.

## Kindaichi's Testimony

The most prominent and prestigious proponent of this particular thesis concerning the difficulty of the Japanese language for the Japanese themselves is the well-known and widely read popularizer of Japanese language scholarship Kindaichi Haruhiko.[1] His little paperback book *Nihongo* (The Japanese language) has been a steady seller since it appeared in 1957. By 1974 it was in its twenty-sixth printing. Kindaichi's book is studded with vivid documentation concerning the ineffability of its subject matter, and this theme of ineffability leads immediately into the theme of difficulty, which is sounded in the first lines of the book's introduction:

> Some people may think that there is nothing at all to writing about the Japanese language. We have lived, using the Japanese language, from the time we were born. They may feel that we ought to be able to write anything and everything at all about the language. But, when we really consider the question, there is nothing as difficult as to write about the Japanese language. It is fairly difficult for us Japanese to find out anything about languages other than Japanese; and that being the case,[2] it is all the more difficult for us to grasp such questions as what is the true essence of the Japanese, or what are its special features. What kind of a language, then, *is* Japanese? This question is a theme in which, despite all these difficulties, we cannot but have great interest.[3]

---

[1] Kindaichi was born in Tokyo in 1913 and graduated from Tokyo University in 1937. He has held a variety of academic positions, including appointments at Nagoya University, the International Christian University (Tokyo), and the Tokyo University of Foreign Studies; he is now on the faculty of the Kyōto Sangyō University.

[2] Here "and that being the case" translates the original's *de aru to sureba*. In all translations of sources and documents in this study (for which, of course, the author is solely responsible) I have tried to pay particular attention to the force of such connective expressions in Japanese syntactic structuring since they very often provide the necessary key to a precise understanding of the direction that the argument of the original is taking. For this reason I have from time to time provided the original Japanese either in a note, as here, or in brackets in the body of the translation to assist the reader who knows the language in the task of correctly interpreting these phrases. For the same reasons, my translations in the present monograph are often more literal, and hence somewhat more wooden, than I would normally tolerate; but it seemed better to err in the direction of being too literal.

[3] Kindaichi Haruhiko, *Nihongo* [The Japanese language], Iwanami shinsho [Iwanami new library], no. 265 (Tokyo: Iwanami Shoten, 1957), p. i. Author's translation.

Kindaichi then continues, in his first chapter, to make it clear to his readers that he is not here referring to the well-known difficulty encountered by foreigners when they attempt to learn Japanese, though, as he is quick to point out, that difficulty too may be documented from official sources. Even at the height of World War II, when the military success of Japanese troops had led to the introduction of the language into certain of the occupied areas of the war theater, official concern was expressed in Japan about the suitability of teaching the language to the occupied foreign populations. The grounds for the concern were the language's well-known difficulty for foreigners, even though they were conquered enemies, and also, somewhat surprisingly, the fear that the language itself might be found wanting in certain important respects.

In this connection, Kindaichi cites a passage from a work by Shimomura Hiroshi written during the period of Japan's military successes:

> Our language is at this very moment expanding overseas, in the wake of the extension of our national destiny, with extraordinary vigor. This is, of course, an unexpected consequence of the progress of the Japanese race; and yet, because of that very fact [*sore dake ni*], it is desirable that the national language of Japan be still more lucid, and still more correct. We are profoundly struck today with the fact that our language is all too chaotic.[4]

This document skirts one of the most important subsidiary sociolinguistic themes, that is, the concept of Japanese as a language simultaneously ineffable and overpowering but, paradoxically enough, at the same time somehow unfit to serve the needs of the society in which it is used and at times even threatening to "come apart" because of its own "special nature." As Kindaichi points out in passing, it is indeed surprising to find this theme in a writing from the time of World War II and in a volume otherwise concerned with presenting Japanese as an "ideal language" (*risōteki na gengo*), a phrase that at the time had become almost a linguistic metaphor for the evident superiority of Japanese military force in the early days of the war in the Pacific theater.

Kindaichi makes it clear, however, that he is talking about something quite different:

---

[4] Shimomura Hiroshi, *Kokugo shinshutsuhen* [The advance of the Japanese language], Kokugo bunka Kōza [Reference series on Japanese language and culture] no. 6; quoted in Kindaichi, *Nihongo*, p. 4. Author's translation.

The "difficulty" of Japanese is not only something having to do with foreigners; it is a language equally as difficult for the Japanese themselves when they study it as it is for foreigners. . . . We must recognize this "difficulty" of Japanese; but we must not feel sorry for ourselves for having inherited this troublesome tongue. A national language is something that is made. Modern German, modern French both have much in them that is artificial.[5]

In Kindaichi's capable hands, this theme now becomes a justification for the very existence of the entire academic discipline of *kokugogaku* ("Japanese language studies") within the Japanese educational and sociocultural structure. He argues that the language is so difficult that the Japanese should attempt to improve upon it, as foreigners have done with their own languages. In order to improve upon it, the Japanese must first know something about their language. In order to know something about it, they must first study its history, its *keitōron*. By definition, however, it is impossible to learn anything about this particular aspect of the problem. Thus, the raison d'être of the entire *kokugogaku* discipline in modern Japanese scholarship, both for serious academic scholars and for popularizers like Kindaichi, may ultimately be referred to this doctrine of the difficulty of the language. This concept is in turn inseparable from the view that the language is ineffable as a mystical experience within the culture.

### Newspaper Accounts

Despite the great amount of attention that Japanese authorities such as Kindaichi provide concerning this facet of the problem, the Japanese reading public also welcomes firsthand testimony from foreigners concerning both the ineffability of the Japanese language and also its difficulty as a medium of human communication. A surprisingly large amount of space is devoted in the daily Japanese press to such accounts, and any attempt to monitor their reportage in this connection soon results in such an overabundance of materials that it is difficult to know which particular article to cite.

A typical specimen may illustrate this genre. An Englishman who

---

[5] Ibid., pp. 5-6. Author's translation.

had just viewed a Japanese movie that was shown in the course of an international summer seminar on communication held in Tokyo is quoted as saying: "Until the day I die, I will never understand why the Japanese use that method of communication of theirs, that method of communication that resembles mental telepathy, accompanying it with only a few words." Immediately following this somewhat cryptic quotation, this newspaper account then added the following editorial opinion: "Yes, certainly, when seen through the eyes of foreigners, this kind of life-attitude of the Japanese [as depicted in the movie under discussion] must appear to be unsettling, and must indeed leave a bad taste." The article from which these two excerpts are taken was accompanied with a photograph showing two young Japanese demonstrating a typical Japanese greeting (*aisatsu*), with both youths bowing slightly toward each other. The demonstration is identified as taking place at the same international seminar before an audience of foreigners who are, it is clear from the photograph, doubled up in uncontrollable laughter. The caption to the photograph reads: "Foreigners laugh uproariously at demonstration of Japanese greetings."[6]

We have already noted above how closely allied to the question of the ineffability of the Japanese language and its consequent difficulty is the issue, so often encountered, of its supposed vagueness or ambiguity. Again, these questions are generally mentioned in the literature as concerns for the Japanese themselves. It is not always easy, however, to keep the domestic strains completely separate from the imported ones, particularly in the modern world of quick travel and telecommunications, where the casual statements of important political figures are immediately transmitted around the world without the safety of the cooling-off periods for reflection and careful retranslation that a more leisurely age often afforded. Both aspects of this question of the ambiguity of Japanese are reflected in a 1973 installment of the popular and widely read column *Tensei jingo* (Voice of the people) which appears daily in the *Asahi Shinbun* (Asahi newspaper). The article shows parallel concern for ambiguity among Japanese and ambiguity resulting from literal translation for the sake of foreigners. The following translation of the article, entitled "Vagueness of Japanese," appeared in the *Asahi Evening News*:

---

[6] *Nihon Keizei Shinbun* [Japanese economic newspaper], July 19, 1972. Author's translation.

If, when one applies for a job, one is told, "Let me think about it," it probably would be natural to consider that there is no hope. If there is no contact after that, it is like a final blow.

However, we have heard that among the young people today, there are those who accept the words at face value and go again to get an answer, asking, "Have you thought about the matter?" Reading the report in Newsweek magazine about the interview with former Prime Minister Eisaku Sato, we felt that the use of words is a very difficult thing. In the interview Mr. Sato touches on the problem of restrictions on textile exports in the meeting with President Nixon. Mr. Sato said, ". . . I did not say that I would do anything specific. Japanese may say, 'I will think about it' and 'I will try to do something about it,' and Americans think we have actually committed ourselves and that some tangible result may come out of it, whereas in Japanese psychology it doesn't mean anything." What happens when an American hears a direct translation of the same words? There were many experts who said, "They would mean that Mr. Sato promised specific steps."

This does not mean that saying things in a roundabout way or obscuring things is not good in all instances. In a country like Japan with only one race, one doesn't have to say things directly to get things across to the other person, and speaking indirectly becomes a wisdom for avoiding friction. An expert in English complained at one time that the Japanese words, "Please do something," when requesting someone to do something, cannot possibly be translated into English.

"Where are you going?" "Just to there." This exchange can be considered to have very meaningless contents, but it serves its purpose. In the case of Mr. Sato, however, there was an illusion in the fact that he thought that the evasive words usually used between Japanese would be understood by Americans. In talking to foreigners, Japanese should speak in very clear-cut terms.[7]

Here we will note that the columnist has touched several important sociolinguistic bases of interest to our study, and we will return to a number of them again. But probably the most striking single point made

---

[7] *Asahi Evening News*, May 7, 1973, translating the column appearing in the previous day's *Asahi Shinbun* [Asahi newspaper]. The article cited was also reprinted in the public relations organ *The Kanagawa*, vol. 20, no. 2 (June-July 1973), and through this source received wide distribution throughout the world.

by the writer is the suggestion that "in talking to foreigners, Japanese should speak in very clear-cut terms." Here we can identify the theme of the difficulty of linguistic contacts with foreigners at its most vivid: it is necessary for the Japanese to use special language when talking to foreigners in Japanese because normal, idiomatic Japanese will necessarily be misunderstood. In the view of the columnist, normal Japanese expression and natural Japanese diction will not be suitable and will probably lead to worse problems than would be brought about by the other extreme of no communication at all.

All this, of course, follows in perfectly logical progression from the a priori assumption of the ineffability and the consequent difficulty of the language. The mystical entity can hardly be allowed to be removed from its sanctuary and shown to foreigners—to uninitiates in the cult—without being changed so as to conceal its true configuration. The real thing is by definition ineffable, so ineffable as to be all but too difficult for the Japanese themselves. The natural conclusion is that only an imitation of the real thing—the Japanese language somehow disguised and altered from its normal diction and expression, a special kind of "very clear-cut" Japanese—should be used when talking to foreigners, even if they do not understand Japanese at all and will have to wait for a translation.

### Suzuki's Testimony

Suzuki Takao's *Tozasareta gengo—Nihongo no sekai* (The world of Japanese—a locked-up language), which appeared in 1975, is a full-length study of what and how the Japanese "feel" about their own language.[8] It is full of new insights in this worked-over field, and in many ways it is the most useful single volume yet to appear in a literature that apparently knows no limits. The volume is remarkable, above everything else, for its author's unwavering determination to approach his chosen subject from fresh angles, even if this means departing

---

[8] Suzuki Takao, *Tozasareta gengo—Nihongo no sekai* [The world of Japanese— a locked-up language] (Tokyo: Shinchōsha, 1975). Suzuki is the author of another book in this field entitled *Kotoba to shakai* [Language and society]. This second book, also published in 1975, similarly deals with questions of the sociolinguistic approach of contemporary Japanese life and culture to problems of the Japanese language, but in a less concentrated fashion. In the present monograph we shall limit ourselves to citations from Suzuki's first 1975 book.

radically from the approaches already canonized by some of the major earlier figures in the field.

Perhaps this totally surprising freshness of his approach may be traced in some measure to his personal background, which is fairly unusual for anyone in Japan writing and working in the field of Japanese sociolinguistics. Suzuki has the usual Japanese academic credentials, but he has also studied and taught in both Canada and the United States and, in addition, has traveled considerably in the Middle East. As a matter of fact, his original field of specialization appears to have been Islamic studies. He has not, however, taught Japanese abroad to foreigners, and so his work does not fall under the ban we imposed in the introduction. He is currently a professor at Keio University's Institute for the Study of Language and Culture. Although this is an important academic post, it is in a private university, and thus he is not bound by the constraints and shibboleths that would go with a more prestigious position within the national university system.

Suzuki can almost always be relied upon to contribute some striking insight into each of the questions that here concern us, and he does not disappoint us on the score of the vagueness and ambiguity of the Japanese language. Although his immediate point of reference in this connection is unfortunately not speech but writing, he has something valuable to contribute.

He begins by citing a pronouncement by a modern French writer and critic to the effect that *ce qui n'est pas clair n'est pas français* ("what is not clear is not French"). He then explores the ramifications of this attitude if it were to be extended to considerations of Japanese prose style:

> I must say that the great majority of the writing by Japan's famous authors and scholars—I am not speaking here of literary compositions as such—seem to be done as if to ensure that they would provide indirect contradiction to [this French author]. Time and time again the reasons and premises for an author's statements are not made clear, and his sentences dissolve into vapidity. [Japanese authors] dislike clarification and full explanation of their views; they like giving dark hints and attempt to leave behind them nuances. But what we must not lose sight of in this connection is the fact that in Japan this is exactly the type of prose that gets the highest praise from readers. Indeed, because readers seek just this kind of writing, and because they enjoy coming into contact with it,

one suspects that this type of prose is, as a result, written more or less intentionally. . . . I think one might very well conclude that, rather than turning away from such writing, Japanese readers instead have a tendency to anticipate with pleasure the opportunities that it will offer them to savor this particular variety of "mystification through language" [*kotoba ni yoru isshu no misuteifuikeishon*].[9]

Suzuki explains the word *mystification* in a parenthetical note as follows: "to become mysterious, or in plain language, to be intoxicated as if enveloped in smoke, or bewitched by a fox."[10]

But there is another side to this matter, as Suzuki himself is quick to admit and explain. He cites at some length a passage in Japanese by a celebrated Japanese scholar of English literature, who is also a well-known and widely read Japanese-language novelist.[11] The cited passage is, beyond any question, a fair specimen of modern Japanese literary criticism; it touches upon Tennyson, Meredith, Browning, Carlyle, and Conrad. Unfortunately, it is totally impossible to reproduce the passage in translation because, as Suzuki himself testifies, it makes almost no concrete sense in Japanese, no matter how often one reads through it. Its nonstop sentences and its almost equally lengthy sentence fragments go smoothly along, held together, indeed more or less cemented to one another, with a variety of syntactic connective tissue. It seems to be language and appears to be a specimen of continuous text. As such, one would expect that it would mean something in Japanese and that that meaning could at least be approximated in a translation. But none of these normal expectations proves justified. As Suzuki puts it:

> As I read through this, attempting to understand what the author is saying, I find myself increasingly puzzled. There is simply too much here that cannot be understood. The passage abounds in expressions that may be taken in any number of meanings, and the relation of sentence after sentence to what goes before or comes after is anything but clear. . . . Since I do not myself pretend to any special literary training, I showed the passage to a friend who is a literary scholar and asked him to read it and tell me what he thought of it. . . . He was not far beyond the first line of the text when already

---

9 Ibid., pp. 31-32. Author's translation.
10 Ibid., p. 32. Author's translation.
11 Ibid., pp. 32-34.

he had arrived at three different opinions about what the author was trying to say.[12]

The type of Japanese prose, particularly scholarly prose, that Suzuki is here illustrating is so dense that in many cases even specialists in the field in question are hard put to answer direct inquiries about just what the text is trying to say about what. It is writing that, since it does not communicate to the reader anything at all about what the author is trying to say, violates the most elementary and functional definition of language as a medium of social interrelationship. Yet, writing of this variety is not only prized by many Japanese scholars and intellectuals but the techniques for its generation are carefully cultivated. Moreover, such writing is widely felt to have a strange and mysterious, but very real, power and strength. In a word, it too is a part, and indeed an important part, of the ineffable process of mystic ecstasy through which modern Japanese sociolinguistic culture views its own language. There is great strength in the unknown; there is even power in the unintelligible. Suzuki continues:

> However, there is a mysterious power [*myō-na chikara*] in this indecipherable passage. As one reads it over and over, one begins to pick up a hint here and a clue there as to what the author was driving at, until suddenly and before one realizes it one can grasp the entire text: how inexplicable [*fushigi*] all this is. . . . In difficulty of this variety, there is something that may be thought of as the covert pleasure that we all feel in pain; and this is what pulls the reader along [*yomu mono wo hikitsukeru*].[13]

It certainly cannot be denied that there is a strong element of masochism in all this. Not everyone will be able to agree out of hand with Suzuki's assumption that there is a "covert pleasure that we all feel in pain." Perhaps the best possible face that can be put onto all this is simply to consider Suzuki's engagingly frank description of his own reactions when confronted with this variety of modern prose. He describes his reactions as a type of "sociolinguistic *Schadenfreude*," in other words, a projection into the sociolinguistic area of those feelings of joy and relief that we all experience upon hearing of the misfortunes of others. Such *Schadenfreude*, at least in its milder manifestations, can

---
[12] Ibid., p. 34. Author's translation.
[13] Ibid., pp. 34-35. Author's translation.

be explained along lines that manage to keep completely clear of the swamps and depths of masochism.

The sociolinguistic correlate of *Schadenfreude*, with which we are involved here, consists of that sense of gratitude and relief that apparently the Japanese reader experiences upon confrontation with texts of the type that Suzuki quotes and comments upon. It is gratitude for the fact that these imponderable difficulties really need not necessarily be puzzled out at all, unless we just happen to wish to try and do so, coupled with relief as the reader realizes that, for the moment at least, they are someone else's concern (in this case, the author's and his publisher's), not ours—after all, we can no more write this kind of text than we can read it. This is probably the most charitable interpretation possible for the emotional response to language of this sort that Suzuki has here cloaked in his somewhat bald confession of "the covert pleasure that we all feel in pain."

The most significant point for us about this passage is neither the precise description of Suzuki's sociolinguistic emotions when faced with pages of practically unintelligible text in his own language, nor even the ultimate sources of his self-admitted feelings of "covert pleasure" that such confrontations generate within him. The point is rather the clearly mystical language in which he has expressed himself upon this entire issue. His description is studded with overt terminology drawn from the technical language of religious mysteries and ecstasy. The most striking instances have been noted in parentheses in the translation above. Both *myō-na* ("mysterious") and *fushigi* ("inexplicable") are, in fact, originally religious terms borrowed into ordinary Japanese from the technical language of Buddhist dialectic. Although the terms have been translated differently above, they both might be rendered simply as "mysterious," in the sense of that which pertains to or partakes of the nature of a religious mystery.

Both of these terms are Chinese loanwords, borrowed into Japanese from the language of Buddhist scriptural texts. They are still redolent of a religious, if not a supernatural or metaphysical, approach to reality. It will be worthwhile to note how these two terms are defined in a recently published Japanese dictionary that attempts to write its definitions "on historical principles."[14] The quasi-adjective *myō* is de-

---

[14] Ōno Susumu, Satake Akihiro, and Maeda Kingorō, *Iwanami kogo jiten* [The Iwanami dictionary of earlier forms of Japanese] (Tokyo: Iwanami Shoten, 1974), p. 6. Author's translation.

fined as follows: "(1) excelling beyond measure; (2) mysterious [*fushigi*] beyond measure; (3) strange, peculiar." This definition, which is found in a Japanese dictionary written solely for the Japanese reader, provides a succinct but complete historical survey of the semantic range of this word in Japanese from the earliest period of the language down to the present. Moreover, it employs the word *fushigi*, another of Suzuki's categorizations in the passage translated above, in order to express its own second meaning for *myō*. This is eloquent testimony to the closeness of the semantic net that binds these two terms together. For its part, the word *fushigi* is defined as follows in the same dictionary: "(1) incapable of comprehension by the intellect; incomprehensible by ordinary cognition; (2) something that ought not properly to exist, unnatural, supernatural; (3) extraordinarily mean, poor." The last of these three meanings is rarely encountered and adds nothing to our present discussion, but the first two show most clearly the religious and mystical aura of both terms.

It would be difficult to ask for a clearer documentation of the Jamesian marks of both the ineffable and the noetic than those provided by this single citation from Suzuki. In addition, he also provides an overt reference to the transient mark in his reference to the instant time dimension in which his mystical experience takes place; "as one reads it over and over, one begins to pick up a hint here and a clue there . . . until suddenly and before one realizes it (*itsu no ma ni ka*). . . ." This is a most precise rendering of the notion of the transient instant during which the overwhelming mystical experience of understanding takes place. Finally, we are told that the reader finds himself "pulled along" (*hikitsukeru*) by the ineffable, noetic, and yet totally transient experience with which the text confronts him. Not only has Suzuki precisely verbalized each of the Jamesian marks of mysticism in describing his own reaction to a difficult Japanese text, but he turns out to have made reference to each of the four marks in the same order in which they appear in James's original presentation. This is surely no accident, since that order is the order of their relative importance, both for understanding the varieties of religious experience, which is what James was concerned with, and for grasping something of the sociolinguistic approach of the contemporary Japanese intellectual to the mystical experience of his own language, which is what Suzuki informs us about.

# 3

# Inadequacies of the Language

Another major theme that can be identified within the sociolinguistic literature can be called "poor-mouthing the Japanese language." At first glance this appears to be in almost direct contradiction to what has been uncovered by our analysis up to this point. Moreover, it is a theme that does not readily fit into the Jamesian framework of mysticism, within which we have until now found such spacious accommodation, although it does shape concepts lying within its borders. This theme finds its most strikingly overt expression in statements or claims to the effect that the Japanese language is a poor language, a weak language, a language lacking in proper grammatical equipment and poor in lexical resources, a language so deficient in all respects that serious proposals have been made more than once in recent Japanese history simply to abandon it altogether and adopt instead some better, richer, stronger language, such as English or French. Yet, this is the same Japanese language that is—by mutual consent of the society if not by definition—ineffable, difficult, and noetic, the same language that transiently exercises a supernatural pulling-power upon its users. The shift in direction is sudden and startling. The adepts in the mystery cult interrupt their ecstasy long enough to suggest that the focus of their mystical activities is hardly worth the trouble they take with it and that it might in fact one day be replaced by a more worthy specimen.

### Suggestions to Replace Japanese

The suggestion to replace Japanese with some other language has been advanced at least twice in recent Japanese history, both times by public figures of such great prestige that their recommendations could not help having a considerable impact, even though in neither case was anything concrete done (nor could it be) to implement their suggestions.

The first such case was that of the Meiji political leader and educator Mori Arinori (1847–1889), who argued in favor of English as a national replacement for Japanese. He went to the length of entering into a correspondence about the subject with William Dwight Whitney at Yale University, then recognized throughout the world as an authority on all sorts of linguistic questions. Mori solicited Whitney's views on whether or not such a switch in national language were as advisable as Mori thought it might be and, if so, how it might best be implemented. Whitney's reply was polite but cautiously, even coolly, negative. Whitney wrote that he had never heard of such a feat being carried off in any other country, and he thought it unlikely that the Japanese could manage it even if it were to their best interests, which he also doubted.[1]

Mori's abortive attempts in this direction were uppermost in the mind of the poet and novelist Shiga Naoya (1883–1972) when he fired the opening salvo in the second of these celebrated "exhortations for the abandonment of the national language" in an article published in April 1946. This was at the very worst point in Japan's post-World War II days. Downtown Tokyo was still a burned-out expanse of wasted city blocks and ruined buildings. Food was scarce and prohibitively expensive. Inflation was rampant. Most of the Japanese population still moved in a kind of sleepwalker's trance, dazed by defeat and stripped of all sense of personal identity. Shiga was so revered as a literary figure during his own lifetime that, as Kindaichi Haruhiko recounts, once when a film clip of him appeared in a prewar newsreel, a student in the movie audience caused a sensation by shouting out the command "Hats off!" He and his companions then stood at bareheaded attention in Shiga's honor. The incident became notorious because the gesture

---

[1] Mori's proposal for the abolition of Japanese and the adoption of English and his correspondence with Whitney are studied and documented in detail in Ivan Parker Hall, *Mori Arinori* (Cambridge, Mass.: Harvard University Press, 1973), pp. 189–195. Of Japanese itself, Mori wrote in 1873 along the following lines: "our meagre language . . . is doomed to yield to the domination of the English tongue, especially when the power of steam and electricity shall have pervaded the land. Our intelligent race . . . cannot depend upon a weak and uncertain medium of communication. . . . The laws of state can never be preserved in the language of Japan. All reasons suggest its disuse."

was one that hinted at extending to Shiga public honors normally extended only to the person of the emperor. Shiga was, as Kindiachi puts it, *shōsetsu no kamisama* ("the deity of fiction").

It is not difficult, then, to understand why the extreme circumstances of Japan in the days immediately following World War II combined with the extraordinary fame of Shiga himself to produce a tremendous popular impact when Shiga published an article that contained passages such as the following:

> We have been accustomed to our present national language since the days of our childhood, and we do not feel all that much in particular about it. But I am of the opinion that there is nothing as imperfect, or as impractical, as the national language of Japan. Once we realize the extent to which the development of our culture has been impeded by this fact, we will also see that here there is a major issue that must by all means be solved on this occasion [Japan's military defeat]. It is no exaggeration to say that unless we achieve such a solution, no hope may be entertained for Japan developing into a genuinely modern nation [*hontō no bunkakoku*]. To document in concrete detail just how imperfect the national language of Japan really is, and to show just how impractical it is, is too vexing a task, and one beyond my abilities; but this is what I have come to feel constantly and most keenly, during my nearly forty years as an author.[2]

We are following Suzuki Takao's selection of the most important portions of Shiga's rather lengthy article. As Suzuki reminds us, the year 1946 was a time when many suggestions were being made for "doing something about the Japanese language." Many of these originated under pressure exerted by the U.S. occupation authorities. Almost all of the suggestions were concerned exclusively with somehow reforming the traditional Japanese orthography, or writing system, in particular

---

[2] Shiga Naoya, "Kokugo undō" [The national language movement], in *Kaizō* [Reconstruction], April 1946; author's translation from the *Kaizō* text of Shiga's article as reprinted in Suzuki, *Tozasareta gengo*, pp. 21ff. There are also excerpts in Kindaichi, *Nihongo*, and in almost every other work of similar nature. The possibility that Shiga's article was intended to be a burlesque of postwar "reform" parties and platforms appears never to have been considered in the Japanese sociolinguistic literature. Everyone now, as then, appears to take everything he says in the *Kaizō* article with complete seriousness.

its use of Chinese characters. Suggestions were even made to abolish the entire inherited writing system and to replace it with romanization.[3]

But, like Mori before him (to whom he made reference in passing), Shiga knew the difference between language and writing. One of the reasons why Shiga's article had such a tremendous impact was that it clearly was the Japanese language itself, and not the writing system, that he was suggesting should be thrown away at this critical juncture in Japanese history. Of course, if the language were to go overboard there would be no problem about the writing system since naturally that would go at the same time:

> More than once during the war, I had occasion to reflect upon the suggestion made sixty years ago by Mori Arinori about adopting English as our national language. I thought about how things might have been if his suggestion had been carried out. One may imagine that Japanese culture [bunka] would surely have advanced far beyond the point where it is today. It occurred to me that most likely a war of the sort we have just been through would never have taken place. And it also occurred to me that then our scholarship would have advanced more easily, and even that we would then have been able to recall our school days as having been something pleasant. We would be like our children who simply have never heard of the cumbersome old Japanese system of arbitrary weights and measures [and hence are at home with the new metric system]. We would not even know our old national language, but we would instead all be speaking English with no consciousness that it was a foreign language, and writing in English. Surely many special words for Japanese situations not to be found today in any English dictionary would have been devised; and I could even conceive of the Man'yōshū and the Genji monogatari being read by far greater numbers of persons than even look at these texts today. . . . And so I got the idea, how would it be if Japan on this occasion [the defeat of 1945] acted with direct and swift resolution, and simply adopted the best language, the most beautiful language in the world, for its national language! I think that French might very well be the best choice. . . . Rather than half-hearted gestures at reform [for example, simply altering the writing system], this action would admit of no possibility of error. . . .

---

[3] See the discussion and sources cited in Roy Andrew Miller, *Bernard Bloch on Japanese* (New Haven: Yale University Press, 1969), pp. xxxviii ff.

I have gotten my idea from Mori Arinori's suggestion for the adoption of English; but I believe that my own plan is a secure one, a thoroughgoing one, and a wise one, far better than any halfhearted, halfway measures of reform, that would only leave us still struggling, for years and even decades ahead, with a maimed national language. I am not at all well-informed about the purely technical aspects of the question of switching from one national language to another, but I do not believe it to be all that difficult. Once the necessary teachers have been trained, I believe that the new language can simply be introduced from the first year of elementary education on.[4]

Suzuki confesses that he, like many younger Japanese intellectuals, had heard about Shiga's attack on the Japanese language but had never really read it until it became necessary to look up the *Kaizō* article in preparation for writing his own book in 1975. He is hard put to conceal the surprise, and indeed the anger, that he felt upon finally coming face-to-face with the infamous passages. Whatever else may be said for or against Shiga's pronouncement, it is an effective piece of writing that obviously still has not lost its power to shock the reader. This continued impact of Shiga's article may be explained in part by reference to almost completely nonlinguistic considerations. The days immediately following the war were so bad that most Japanese who lived through them have allowed memory to draw that convenient veil that it eventually always provides in order to protect us from the recollection of most thoroughly unpleasant and unrewarding episodes, in national life as in private affairs. Others, too young at the time to have their own reliable direct recollection of those days, have an even less distinct impression of the way things were, since their memories are adulterated by the semiromanticized versions of events that they have pieced together from secondhand accounts. For both groups, however, reading Shiga's violent outburst against this central element in the entire mystique of Japanese cultural structuring brings back the disillusion and the despair of 1945–1946 in all too vivid detail.

## Japanese as Imperfect and Impractical

Of course, nothing was done to implement Shiga's suggestions, any more than anything had been done to carry out Mori's ideas. But this

---

[4] Suzuki, *Tozasareta gengo*, pp. 23-24. Author's translation.

does not mean that Shiga's broadside on the language was soon forgotten or that it has been without continuing influence in the consideration of sociolinguistic questions in the literature in Japan. Although there was not the least enthusiasm for implementing his recommendations for language transplant, the charges that Shiga leveled against the Japanese language found a ready audience, and they continue to be popular. Two of the charges in particular were embodied, in the *Kaizō* article, in terms that continue to appear in the sociolinguistic literature with surprising persistence. These are Shiga's charges that the Japanese language is *fukanzen* ("imperfect," with further implications of incomplete, unfinished, defective in workmanship or manufacture) and that it is also *fuben* ("impractical," with implications of inconvenient, tedious, old-fashioned, as for example might be said of cooking over a charcoal brazier instead of a gas range). These two categorizations, *fukanzen* and *fuben*, turn up with surprising regularity in the post-Shiga sociolinguistic literature. They have become the canonical terms for reference to various elements in, and aspects of, the Japanese language that are identified as being potential trouble spots within the linguistic structure, especially with respect to this structure's role in a modern industrial society. We have come a long way from the hushed temple of mysteries, and even the most devout members of the cult find it difficult to ignore the thrust and impact of Shiga's attack.

Kindaichi, for example, begins his classic primer on the Japanese language with a brief allusion to Shiga. He comments: "Today, ten years after the war, the Japanese language is as alive and well as ever. The voices urging us to adopt French or something else have simply faded away, and today they serve only as the themes for stories that we tell about 'the old days'—which is just as it should be."[5] But Kindaichi does not get very far into his book before he himself is busy drawing up a "Syllabus of Defects" of the Japanese language.[6] Using the term *fuben*, he even indulges in such section headings as "The Impracticability of [Japanese word order in which] Attributes Come First, and its Remedies" and "The Impracticability of Predicates Coming Last."[7]

In the section entitled "Japanese Viewed from its Vocabulary," Kindaichi rehashes in turn a large number of the charges of imperfec-

---

[5] Kindaichi, *Nihongo*, p. 2. Author's translation.
[6] Ibid., pp. 98ff.
[7] Ibid., p. 16. Author's translation.

46

tion and impracticability that have been leveled against the language in the sociolinguistic literature, and he adds his own interpretation to these charges. He begins with a citation from the *Bunshō tokuhon* (A manual of prose style) by the modern literary giant Tanizaki Jun'ichirō (1886–1965):

> One of the defects [*ketten*] of our national language is the fact that its vocabulary is limited. . . . For example, we refer to the revolving of a child's top, or of a mill wheel, or of the earth around the sun, all with the same words, *mawaru* or *meguru*. . . . This poverty of the Japanese vocabulary is evidence of the fact that our national character does not esteem chattering.[8]

The theme of alleged Japanese reluctance to verbalize is a popular one, both in the sociolinguistic literature and in certain types of contemporary literary criticism, in which one even finds mention of "the typical Japanese dislike of the verbal." The following passage can serve as an example from a work of literary criticism:

> It might be said that the culture is primarily visual, not verbal, in orientation, and social decorum provides that reticence, not eloquence, is rewarded. . . . Silence not only invites and seduces all would-be speakers and writers, but is in fact a powerful compulsion throughout the whole society.[9]

Clearly this theme contradicts much of what we have already learned about the sociolinguistic literature and the enormous interest in verbalization of all varieties that it reflects within modern Japanese society. This is only one example of the network of internal contradictions in the literature.

In explanation of Tanizaki's blunt statement, Kindaichi suggests that "he is only criticizing the Yamato words in the Japanese language."[10] Kindaichi goes on to suggest that Tanizaki's criticism is wide of the mark if applied to the language as a whole because the limited

---

[8] Ibid., p. 98. Author's translation. Here Tanizaki uses the expression *o-shaberi de nai*, literally "is not voluble, does not chatter, talk lightly," with *o-shaberi*, a deverbal noun from *shaber-u*, "to chatter, patter," originally a semihumorous sound-imitative word, but now in the modern Tokyo language almost synonymous with *hanas-u*, the normal word for "to speak," and having only the very slightest semantic differences with that more formal term.
[9] Masao Miyoshi, *Accomplices of Silence, the Modern Japanese Novel* (Berkeley: University of California Press, 1974), p. xvi.
[10] Kindaichi, *Nihongo*, p. 98. Author's translation.

47

resources of the Yamato vocabulary are now pieced out by large-scale borrowings of loanwords from many sources, particularly Chinese.

With such an explanation we have come full circle, only to end up in a logical cul-de-sac. If we accept Kindaichi's explanation, the Yamato words that Tanizaki was criticizing are the same Yamato words that are said to constitute the mystical core of the language and to transmit the essential message of national, cultural, and racial identity. In this role they have been carefully identified and preferred over all loanwords, particularly over loanwords from Chinese, which have been held to be totally incapable of any such mission of cultural identity and transmission. Indeed, so important is the supposed role of the Yamato level of the vocabulary that we have seen it being defended even against quite positive philological evidence that indicates how it too is shot through with early loans from foreign languages. But now it is this same Yamato level of the language's lexical resources that Kindaichi immediately abandons to the attack of Tanizaki, without even the pretence of a refutation of his charges.

Kindaichi continues his discussion of Yamato words and their problems with a quotation from still another literary giant, this time the poet Hagiwara Sakutarō (1886–1942):

> Yamato words are extremely aesthetic, but they are too feeble for occasions when we would express anger, distress, jealousy, and similar strong emotions. The Yamato words are poor in the elements that would express such accents [akusento], but by using Chinese words, strong accents may be expressed. Thanks to the simplicity and strength of Chinese words, we are able to give strong expression to human emotions.[11]

With this, we have landed back squarely into the dialectic of Watanabe Shōichi's argument already explored in Chapter 1. We have noted how Watanabe, while stressing the ineffability and other mystical marks of the Yamato words in the Japanese lexicon, was at the same time completely willing to write off the literal intellectual content of the literary monuments preserved in (and preserving) these same Yamato words. He did not scruple to term a famous Man'yōshū poem full of Yamato words "almost equal in quality to a scribble a middle school child on a school excursion might make on a postcard for home."

---

[11] Ibid., p. 22. Author's translation.

The alleged lack of objective intellectual quality and the apparent total absence of translatable content are for Watanabe not defects but the key arguments bolstering his thesis concerning the spirit of the language and its communication through imperceptible channels.

It would be misleading to leave the impression that Kindaichi endorses all the allegations of imperfectness and impracticability that he catalogues and documents from the sociolinguistic literature. Often he takes issue with the critics of the language and, in balance, the total theme of his book is a measured defense of the language against its domestic critics. He is arguing, in effect, that Japanese is not all *that* imperfect, not all *that* impracticable; in sum total, it is not really as bad as many of its critics have suggested.

For our present investigation the most significant issue is, however, not what Kindaichi argues in any particular case or allegation, but the very fact that he finds it necessary to undertake these arguments at all. He takes these charges against the Japanese language very seriously, as does the contemporary sociolinguistic literature as a whole. He is clearly motivated in all this by the fact that these charges and allegations have been made not only by sociolinguistic popularizers like himself but also by important figures with tremendous cultural and literary reputations, such as Hagiwara, Tanizaki, and especially Shiga. Attacks from such prestigious quarters must be answered, or the battle will be lost by default.

It is also significant to note how often Kindaichi himself admits the validity of these allegations, especially when they have been made by persons who are highly respected within the Japanese cultural system. One such person is the all-but-sainted founder of folklore studies in Japan, Yanagita Kunio (1875–1962), whom Kindaichi quotes to the following effect:

> Modern Japanese has a poverty-stricken vocabulary; it has many words, but they all incline in one direction. It is also poor in the types of syntactic structures available, so that in putting together a moderately long sentence, everyone has had the experience of not being able to come up with anything except something that is dull and boring.[12]

Yanagita is revered as the champion, if not the rediscoverer, of almost everything truly and essentially Japanese, whether the field be

---

[12] Ibid., p. 100. Author's translation.

folklore, folk art, cultural history, or any other manifestation of the true, native Japanese spirit and expression. A charge from such an exalted quarter must necessarily draw an unusual response, and Kindaichi does not disappoint us. He cites in refutation a passage from the French philosopher Lucien Lévy-Bruhl (1857–1939) to the general effect that the language of a social entity in the "prelogical" stage is distinguished by an almost complete lack of terms for generalized or abstract concepts. Instead, such a language has a large resource of specific terms that immediately "depict" carefully delimited individual entities, be they persons, objects, or whatever. Kindaichi does not venture upon a discussion of just how Lévy-Bruhl arrived at this point of view, or of what his sources for society in its "prelogical" stages were. Indeed, little of what the French scholar has to say in this connection would stand very close scrutiny from the point of view of linguistic science.[13] Kindaichi's gambit is a far simpler one: balance a distinguished Japanese critic with a distinguished foreign one, and let them shoot it out for themselves, even though the result may very well prove to be little more conclusive than the proverbial Mexican standoff. Kindaichi argues that, in the terms of the Lévy-Bruhl formulation, Japanese is surely not underdeveloped since it has, and always has had, such generalized terms as *mono* ("thing") and *koto* ("fact"), as well as such useful syntactic devices for abstract discourse as the topic marker *wa* and the copula *da*. He concludes his discussion as follows:

> At least on these points, the view that Japanese is less theoretical than the languages of Europe cannot be maintained; and though it is, to be sure, with considerable hesitation that I do this [*hanahada enryō shinagara de wa aru ga*], I would recommend Japanese as being in actual point of fact rather more theoretical than those other languages, contrary to what is generally believed.[14]

Here Kindaichi's elaborate protestations of hesitation (*enryō*) are of course explained by the fact of Yanagita's tremendous reputation in Japanese cultural and intellectual circles. One does not lightly under-

---

[13] Lévy-Bruhl, in his *Les Fonctions mentales dans les sociétés inférieures* (1910), originally held that there was an essential difference between primitive and civilized thought and stressed the notion of a "prelogical" quality to the "primitive mentality." But he himself later agreed with the critics who pointed out that the term "prelogical" tended to confuse psychological and cultural data.
[14] Kindaichi, *Nihongo*, p. 101. Author's translation.

take to contradict in public the pronouncements of such a man as Yanagita. In fact, Kindaichi continues on the next page of his book to try and soften the impact of his disagreement with Yanagita somewhat. Elsewhere Yanagita had complained about the scarcity of adjectives in Japanese, and Kindaichi proves himself almost eager to support this particular allegation, even illustrating it with his own example. Japanese, he says, lacks a good adjective meaning "to have an odor," referring to odor in general. The most usual word in this semantic area is *kusai* ("to stink") and there is also *kōbashii*, used of the aroma of newly roasted tea leaves. But he admits the lack of a word meaning simply "to have an odor," and he finds this impractical (*fuben*).[15]

### Suggestions to Adopt Japanese

This chapter began with an account of some historic Japanese suggestions concerning the adoption of another, totally different, language in place of Japanese. There have also been hints from time to time in recent history of the opposite process—the adoption of Japanese by foreign countries, or at least by foreign social entities, either as a replacement for a European language or as an auxiliary instrument to be used alongside some other linguistic vehicle. The most important example of this comes from the attempts made during World War II to introduce Japanese into the temporarily occupied areas of the war theater. This remains a rich field for future study, but it is outside the scope of our present investigation. We can, however, hardly pass on to other facets of our problem without at least a glance at a recent document that falls into this last category. It is from a 1974 issue of the *Daily Yomiuri*:

> It is said that as many as 1,500 reporters from many countries in the world are covering the seventh summit meeting of Arab heads of state which is being held to debate the issue of Palestine representation. . . .
> Usually, either English or French is used as the official language at an international conference. . . .
> But this is not the case with the Arab summit meeting.
> The chiefs of state and other officials of Arab countries attending the meeting speak in the Arabic language at press conferences.

---

[15] Ibid., p. 102.

51

Pamphlets and other printed matter concerning the meeting are also written in Arabic. . . .

The fact that Arabic is being used as the official language at the Arab summit meeting may reflect the growing nationalism of Arab countries, which say in effect: "If you want to listen to us, study the Arabic language." . . .

Starting with this year's UN General Assembly session, Arabic became the sixth official language of the world organization. . . .

The other five official languages of the UN are English, French, Spanish, Russian, and Chinese.

These are the languages of the countries which have large spheres of influence.

Some people hold that Japanese should be made an official language of the UN too.

Education Minister Seisuke Okuno, who attended the recent general meeting of the UNESCO . . . said at a cabinet meeting that he wished that Japanese would be made an official language at international organizations. Some other cabinet ministers reportedly agreed with Okuno's idea.

If a language has real power which nobody can disregard and is closely associated with a charming and profound culture, many people will study that language without being asked to do so.

If we try to force our language on people in other countries, they will not understand our true intentions and might even misunderstand us. The problem of the relationship between languages and nationalism is one which is worthy of study.[16]

The speculations of the *Yomiuri* writers require no elaborate comment, except to note in passing that they too, in the last analysis, conclude their statement with a classic reference to the passive mark of the mystical experience. They allude to a language that "has real power which nobody can disregard. . . ."

---

[16] *Daily Yomiuri*, November 1, 1974; the article originally appeared in Japanese in the *Yomiuri Shinbun* [Yomiuri newspaper], October 29, 1974.

# 4
# The Writing System

William James's mark of the noetic quality of the mystical experience—that "overwhelming experience of understanding" carrying with it "a curious sense of authority for aftertime"—is the best theoretical construct available to us to explain the sheer bulk of what we are calling the contemporary Japanese sociolinguistic literature. Just as the experience itself is overwhelming in the understanding it carries, so is the literature describing this experience overwhelming in its quantity and diversity.

This mark of the noetic must also be kept in mind if we are to begin to understand the underlying basis for what might otherwise appear to be a curious, if not a fatal, contradiction. On the one hand, there is the often-repeated testimony in the literature affirming and exploring the ineffable quality of the language, but, on the other hand, there is the considerable bulk of that literature itself. This voluminous literature has as its only goal explicating the subtleties of the Japanese language in great detail. In a word, it goes to great lengths to describe the undescribable, to express the ineffable.

This situation actually is paradoxical, not contradictory. It has a direct parallel in the dialectic of the Zen school of Buddhism. On the one hand, Zen assures us that all written texts are hardly worth the paper that they are written upon. As an illustration of this, an exquisite and often-reproduced early Chinese Zen painting shows one of the first Zen masters gleefully ripping up roll after roll of scriptural texts. On the other hand, the Zen school has traditionally devoted enormous amounts of effort and study to the exegesis and collation of a number of important Buddhist canonical texts. The issue is one of balance, proportion, and priorities; it simply cannot be approached along the lines of traditional Western ideas of exclusivity. One approach does not necessarily rule out the other.

The Zen schools are perfectly sincere in their insistence upon the triviality of written texts; they assign much greater weight to the oral transmission of their message through the personal teachings of priests in the direct line of clerical succession. But that does not mean that Zen does not also devote considerable attention to those same texts; after all, their true triviality will be fully apparent only when the texts are thoroughly understood. Only then can they be measured against the oral tradition, and only then will we be in a position to understand just how greatly they are wanting.

In much the same way, in contemporary sociolinguistic literature the a priori assumption of ineffability renders trivial by comparison any attempts to explain the language and literature, but that does not mean that these attempts will or should be neglected. Indeed, because the experience of ineffability is itself so overwhelming, we cannot help but make every possible effort to describe the indescribable, if only in a kind of lingering tribute that itself becomes a metaphor for the lingering sense of authority that the mystical experience of the language initially introduces. No mystical experience can long be maintained, but its sense of authority does linger, and so does the explanatory literature that it generates.

## Enduring Authority

In the case of Japanese, this lingering sense of authority finds another virtually automatic metaphor in the inherited writing system. Language is by its essence a fleeting, naturally transient phenomenon. Hence it is ideally suited for its role in traditional Japanese culture as the prime vehicle for the implementation of the mystical experience. The spoken word is the most transient of all sociological transactions. In fact, with the single exception of language, every mode of cooperation in the social entity leaves behind it substantial evidence that is more or less lasting in nature—for example, families, buildings, artifacts, even continuing patterns of traditional behavior. With spoken language, no traces remain. Only through writing do we have the possibility of generating permanent residues—documents, texts, books—that will survive as concrete correlates of the linguistic act. In the case of Japanese, such permanent residues of course take the form of written records employing the traditional writing system, which is a curious mixture of Chinese characters with Japanese syllabic-phonetic symbols.[1]

The written records themselves thus become prime targets for secondary sociolinguistic speculation and comment of all types— secondary because the speculation deals not directly with language but with the form in which the language appears in written records. At the same time, written records naturally become areas for the implementation of authority because all orthographies, or writing systems, by their very nature incorporate a large number of purely arbitrary features. There are always some aspects of a writing system that simply must be learned and remembered, even though we already know the language. Sometimes these things can be very few in number, and learning the writing will therefore be, for native speakers of the language at least, comparatively easy. In other systems the items that must be learned by rote, and that have little if any connection with the language itself, can reach very great numbers, making the time and effort that must be spent in order to learn to read and write the language great. How to spell this or that word, how to write this or that morphological ending, what combination of punctuation to use when any one of several possible combinations would serve equally well—decisions such as this can only be made in an arbitrary, authoritarian way. Such decisions are almost always presented in terms of right and wrong, but they are arbitrary decisions and can only be learned by rote. Writing systems linger on, established and continued by the inherent implementation of arbitrary authority. In the difficult Japanese writing system, and in its written records, we find a concrete, physical expression for that lingering sense of authority that accompanies all mystical experiences.

Indeed, a significantly large portion of the sociolinguistic literature deals exclusively with the problems and questions that arise in the daily application of the inherited writing system to the Japanese language and with questions concerning its proposed, or possible, reform. Much of what is written about language reform in modern Japan turns out on closer inspection actually to deal not with language at all but rather with changes in the writing system. The bulk of the deliberations of

---

[1] For an account of the Japanese writing system and its development that is written with the idea of making it possible for a reader interested in this question to follow the discussion without knowing either Japanese or Chinese characters, see Miller, *Japanese Language*, pp. 90ff.

the *Kokugo shingikai* ("National Language Council"), an official, cabinet-level, consultative organ of the Japanese government, are concerned with questions, not of language, but of script, despite its name.[2] As such, these orthographic questions are not of immediate concern in the present study, in which we are primarily interested in language itself. But one segment of the treatment of these issues in the literature does have significant sociolinguistic aspects and deserves mention, particularly since it exemplifies the attempts in the literature to justify the inherited Japanese writing system and to make for it claims of positive superiority over other, simpler writing systems, typically claims of superiority over the alphabetic writing systems of the West. Such allegations are, on their very face, so extraordinary that they deserve some notice.

Anyone attempting to justify the modern Japanese writing system has his work cut out for him, to say the least. It is not impossible to learn the writing system; the Japanese learn it, and so do a few foreigners. It is not impossible to apply it to a modern, industrial, telecommunications-oriented society; Japan has developed the technological implementations that are necessary in order to employ the inherited writing system in contemporary economic and social activities. But the writing system used in Japan, mixing Chinese characters with phonetic syllabary symbols, is cumbersome and costly. It is being perpetuated in a world for which it was not designed.

Nevertheless, this writing system is a fact of modern Japanese social and cultural life, and it is not in the least likely to change or be changed in any important respect in our lifetimes. Suggestions for radical script reform in modern Japan now come only from genuine fringe groups. Japanese society has encountered, and has survived, three major historical catastrophes which shook it to its foundations. The

---

[2] The *Kokugo shingikai* [National language council] was established by a cabinet directive in 1949 and defined as "an organ to carry out studies and discussions on matters relating to the reform of the national language, the advancement of national language education, and romanization, as well as to make recommendations to the Minister of Education on items relating to those matters that it deems essential." Quoted in Kokugo gakkai [Japanese language association], ed., *Kokugogaku jiten* [Dictionary of Japanese language studies], 17th ed. rev. (Tokyo: Tōkyōdō, 1969), p. 419. The inclusion of "romanization" as one of the primary official concerns of this deliberative and consultative organ of the Ministry of Education provides striking primary documentation for the concern about script reform and the vigor with which the now-dead issue of romanization was still being debated in the first years following the defeat.

first of these, the Taika Reform of the late seventh century, helped set the course of the society toward the introduction of Chinese script from the continent, and it is these imported orthographic elements that still form the heart of the writing system. The question of abandoning the entire writing system arose during the two subsequent catastrophes, the Meiji Restoration (1868–1912) and the defeat in World War II; but in both instances it was firmly rejected. Having survived this much in the past, there seems little reason to imagine that the script will prove vulnerable to social or cultural forces dictating change in the immediate future.

## Experience of Understanding

Suzuki Takao devotes a large portion of his book to discussion of the writing system. Although most of this discussion has little bearing on sociolinguistic questions, he does become involved in an elaborate defense of the use of the traditional script that is interesting since it hinges upon the most commonly encountered theme of the literature in this area. This theme might be paraphrased along these lines: "We understand our language better than you do yours, thanks to the fact that we write ours with Chinese characters and you do not."

What Suzuki and the others who allude to this theme in their writing are driving at is roughly the following: because the Chinese characters used in writing Japanese serve as discrete symbols for the individual morphemes (the smallest discrete unit of a language), these writers claim that long Chinese compounds written in a Japanese text are more easily understood by the average reader than are similarly long compounds based upon Latin or Greek borrowings, given a reader of equal educational level in Europe or America.

The specific example that Suzuki gives will clarify his reasoning on this issue.[3] He cites the case of a British typist of no particular educational accomplishments who might very well not understand just what the English word *anthropology* meant if she encountered it in something that she had been given to type. Suzuki argues that her Japanese equivalent would do better with the Japanese word *jinruigaku* ("anthropology") because of the way in which a word like this is written in Japanese. By simply looking at the way in which *jinruigaku* is written

---

[3] Suzuki, *Tozasareta gengo*, p. 86.

in the Japanese text, he argues, the Japanese typist would be able to guess what the word means. This, he suggests, means that Japanese writing, far from being cumbersome or troublesome, is actually far superior to the way in which the languages of Europe are written.

The modern Japanese word *jinruigaku* is a neologism formed by putting together borrowed Chinese roots, much as *anthropology* is an English neologism coined from Greek roots. Suzuki argues that his uneducated Japanese typist would immediately, clearly, and effectively grasp what the term *jinruigaku* means and what the science it names is all about and hence would be head and shoulders above her British counterpart. The Japanese writing system will write the first morpheme *jin* with the Chinese character for *man*, the second morpheme *rui* with the character for *category*, and the third morpheme *gaku* with the character for *study*. From this, the Japanese typist is supposed to be able to understand what anthropology is and what it studies.

One can easily take issue with Suzuki's formulation. The question remains, How much does putting together a string of individual morphemes like "man-category-study" tell anyone about the discipline of anthropology? What the Chinese script does in such an instance is to remind the reader of the etymology of a given word. Although this may be interesting, it is not, in and of itself, a sure guide either to the meaning of the word or to its usage. Etymologies tell us about the histories of words—where they came from, how they were made up—but not about what they mean or how we use them.

Another problem that makes the example selected by Suzuki rather less than convincing has to do with the word *jinruigaku* itself. The term was coined in Japan several generations ago to describe anthropology viewed chiefly as a science for measuring and cataloging physical distinctions among different human specimens (hence *rui*, "category," in the word). It is used today in Japanese educational circles for all varieties of anthropology, including cultural and social anthropology, but Japanese scholars agree that it is something of a linguistic anachronism, since it was coined to describe a kind of anthropology that is increasingly rare in Japan, as in the West. This means that, even if the Japanese typist of Suzuki's example should be able to put together the morphemes of *jinruigaku* correctly and manage to guess that the word means the science of categorizing or classifying men, she would still be somewhat far from the mark of what the word probably means in the particular text that she has been given to work with. It is difficult to agree that

58

the typist has received any particular help from the inherited Japanese writing system.

But for Suzuki, his hypothetical Japanese typist is a way of "proving" that the inherited Japanese system of writing is not, as most would argue, a burden upon both the society and the culture, but rather a positive boon to both. In fact, he argues that it is a boon with certain democratic implications: "The fact that the Japanese language uses a liberal number of Chinese characters . . . is a major factor that has prevented high-level concepts and difficult words from becoming the exclusive property of a limited, especially privileged class."[4]

Few would be able to agree with this statement. But it does have its value, if only because such exceptionally direct presentations of this particular point of view are comparatively rare in the sociolinguistic literature. This argument contrasts directly with that made by Watanabe Shōichi in the *Japan Echo* article. Watanabe argued that the ancient Japanese possessed a "living language" of Yamato words which could be easily understood and used by all, but that the Chinese words and characters made language mastery possible only for the elite.

Starting from the same materials, Suzuki and Watanabe have ended up with diametrically opposed conclusions. For Suzuki, the use of Chinese characters in the script is a factor in social leveling and something that prevents the development of an educated elite in sole possession of the meanings and utility of difficult words such as *jinruigaku*. For Watanabe, the existence of Chinese neologistic loanwords such as *jinruigaku* is an indication that contemporary Japanese is a "dead" language when viewed alongside such "living" languages as the Yamato vocabulary elements in Japanese, with their immediate, if mystic, comprehensibility. The differences in their two positions appear to be irreconcilable.

---

[4] Ibid.

# 5

# A Modern Threat to the
# Ancient Language

Mystic states of ecstasy seem, by their very nature, impossible to sustain for more than a short period of time; from this follows the third of the Jamesian marks, that of being transient. But this limitation is more than balanced by the ready possibility that the afterglow resulting from the overwhelming experience of understanding may very well persist for a lifetime. In the mystical experience of the Japanese language, this lifetime extends far beyond the biological lifetime of any individual speaker; it tends to become longer and longer until eventually it is so extended that it is, in effect, coextensive with the lifetime of the entire culture that employs it. The afterglow is, in a word, as durable as Japan itself.

This phenomenon of perpetual afterglow in the contemporary sociolinguistic approach of Japanese intellectual circles toward the Japanese language can most readily be documented from many of the general statements of purpose and intent with which a number of prominent scholars of the language, particularly scholars of the Tokyo school with special interests in the problems of the history of the language, often preface their work. Many examples could be cited, but a few drawn from the writing of Ōno Susumu will provide a representative sampling.[1]

---

[1] Ōno was born in Tokyo in 1919 and graduated from Tokyo University in 1943. He is a professor at the Gakushuin University in Tokyo. His serious scholarly reputation in Japan, which is considerable, is largely based upon his early work in the phonology of Old Japanese and his annotations to the Iwanami Shoten's edition of the *Man'yōshū* [Anthology of a myriad leaves] published in its Nihon koten bungaku taikei [Corpus of Japanese classical literature] series between 1957 and 1962.

## Ōno's Approach to the History of Japanese

For some years Ōno has been occupied, in collaboration with two other scholars, Satake Akihiro and Maeda Kingorō, in the compilation of a dictionary of older forms of the Japanese language. In late November 1974 he published a paperback summing up in extremely readable form his views on many questions about the history of Japanese. Ōno's little paperback made the Japanese best-seller lists for several weeks and certainly more than served its primary purpose of drumming up business for the dictionary itself.

An important feature of the Ōno dictionary is the large-scale attempt that it makes to provide etymologies for many of the words that it lists, particularly for the words that Ōno considers to be "basic vocabulary." He does this in a few cases by citing forms from Korean that he thinks may be genetically related to the Japanese forms in question. More often, however, he attempts to evolve an etymology for a given Japanese form totally within Japanese without reference to other languages. Few of Ōno's attempts in this last direction will be of interest to the linguist, either the specialist in Japan or the foreign scholar, because they seldom rise above the level of clever folk etymology. A discussion of the methodological failings of this aspect of Ōno's work would take us too far afield here, but the reasons he gives for what he does are of considerable documentary value for a study of contemporary Japanese sociolinguistic approaches.

In the introduction to his paperback, Ōno begins with the following passage:

> In each of the various countries of the world, different styles of life obtain, and different languages are used; furthermore, in these,[2] there are different traditions of thought. In the midst of these, what is the way of looking at things, the way of thinking, of the Japanese? Also, what is the power [*chikara*] that lies at the basis [*soko*] of the actions of modern Japanese and that controls their way of thinking in an invisible fashion [*mienai tokoro de*]? Is it not true that within our way of looking at things, and within our way of thinking, both of which have been handed down unconsciously from the remote

---

[2] In Ōno's original, it is not clear whether "these" should be taken as having reference to "these various countries" or to "these different languages." Most likely the second was intended.

past, there may well be something surprisingly deep-rooted that still exercises its power over modern man? Ancient Japan is so far removed from us today as to seem to be virtually without any relationship to us; however, in actual fact, I suspect that there are instances in which it is still living in the present, in fresh and vital forms.[3]

By this time we are familiar with the frame of analysis which makes it possible to understand Ōno's references to "the power that lies at the basis of the actions of modern Japanese" and that, from there, manages to control "their way of thinking in an invisible fashion" (or, somewhat more literally, "from some locus that is invisible"). Again, explicit reference is made to the traits that James found indicative of a mystical experience.

It remains only to note that by "Ancient Japan" (*kodai Nihon*) Ōno makes it clear that he does not mean what in linguistic scholarship is generally called the Old Japanese period—that is, the earliest period for which we have substantial written records, the period of the court at Nara (710–784):

> "Ancient Japan" means Japan before written records. How did the people of Japan of that period view their own world? What did they believe, what did they fear, what did they hold to be happiness? In other words, what were the foundations of Japanese culture? I would like to discover as much as possible about all these things.[4]

With this definition, Ōno removes his studies from the horizons of linguistic methodology and relocates them in the midst of the game of speculation and introspective estimates about what preliterate man may have thought, or may have wished for, or may have feared. Since his field of inquiry is to be the preliterate culture of Japan and the psychology of the preliterate Japanese, there will be no possibility of documenting any of the theories that he may evolve with citations from written sources. It will never be possible to suggest that anything he may come up with in the way of speculative insight might be more convincing if it could somehow be documented, because nothing in the entire system can possibly be documented. By the same token, no specu-

---

[3] Ōno Susumu, *Nihongo wo sakanoboru* [Tracing back the history of Japanese], Iwanami shinsho, no. 911 (Tokyo: Iwanami Shoten, 1974), p. 1. Author's translation.
[4] Ibid. Author's translation.

lation or intuitive formulation can possibly be ruled out because no evidence can be offered for or against any view that Ōno may wish to advance. Thus, little of what Ōno is doing will be of interest to the serious linguist concerned with the history of the Japanese language, but the way in which he is doing it is of primary relevance for the study of the sociolinguistic orientation of a representative contemporary Japanese intellectual vis-à-vis his own language.

In the introduction to the new dictionary itself, Ōno provides further important insights into both the sociolinguistic approach he uses and that of the school in which he is such a key figure:

> Anyone who is a Japanese sees before his eyes the learning and technology of Europe and America when he awakens to the world of the intellect. Many people believe that opening up the future for Japan consists in studying and adopting these. However, what in the world really *is* a Japan that concentrates on studying Europe and America? There are many ways in which to investigate the sources of the ideology and culture of Japan. Among these, I have chosen the way of learning about Japan by explaining the Japanese language.[5] In order to discover clearly the ultimate origins of the Japanese language,[6] I have considered it a vital task to study Ancient Japanese, and as a development from that, to learn about the genetic relationship and development of Japanese. . . .[7]

With this passage we are suddenly introduced to one of the most important minor themes in the entire body of the contemporary sociolinguistic literature. Ōno refers to the study of Japanese and its origins as an alternative to the study of the West and of Western learning and technology for the modern Japanese intellectual. What kind of a Japan in reality is it, Ōno asks here, if it is to be simply a Japan that concentrates all its abilities and energies on studying and learning from the

---

[5] Or, somewhat more literally, "by making the Japanese language clear [*Nihongo wo akiraka ni suru*]."

[6] Again, a less than ideal translation for a passage that is anything but smooth in the original: *Nihongo no kongen wo akiraka ni shiru tame ni* . . . Here *kongen* ("ultimate origins") is not a technical linguistic term, but simply a general and quite vague lexical item. The variation back and forth between technical terminology and general expressions is one of the stylistic hallmarks of this variety of the sociolinguistic literature; needless to say, it renders the task of a translator even more difficult than it generally is in this area.

[7] Ōno, Satake, and Maeda, *Iwanami kogo jiten*, p. i. Author's translation.

West? The strong implication of his heavily ironic rhetoric in this passage is that it is not much of a place—in particular, it is not much of a place for the Japanese intellectual.

Where can the Japanese scholar turn if he is to find worthwhile intellectual activities that can be carried on in isolation from the learning and technology of the West? The following anecdote might help to put the question in perspective. In the last years of the Tokugawa period, Sakuma Shōzan (1811–1864) tried to construct a cannon following not only the instructions in the imported Dutch books on metallurgy but also the neo-Confucian metaphysical constructs embodied in certain arcane interpretations of the hexagrams in the *I Ching* (Book of changes). His was a valiant early attempt to combine Eastern ethics with Western technology; unfortunately it was also a failure. The weapon exploded the first time it was fired.[8] Where can the modern Japanese intellectual turn in order to find a field of academic endeavor that may be pursued by a Japanese operating solely as a Japanese, free of any infusion of Western learning and technology, so as to avoid the possibility of being blasted to bits when the entire apparatus explodes? To the study of the Japanese language and its most remote origins, of course.

To carry out such study in these carefully delimited terms will mean that Western linguistic science, its techniques and methodology, will have to be isolated from the study of Japanese as far as possible. But surely this is a small price to pay for the successful establishment of an entire new field of academic learning—one hesitates to denominate it a discipline—that may be safely pursued in total and comfortable isolation from the West. Let the Japanese scholars of English, French, and even Chinese concern themselves with foreign linguistic "learning and technology"; the scholar of Japanese is free to go his own way— as Ōno goes his, both in his paperback and in his dictionary.

### The West as Corrupter of Japanese

At this point, the sociolinguistic literature begins to converge with a far greater body of writing in modern Japan, writing in which the West appears preeminently as a metaphor for the rapidly escalating corrup-

---

[8] Charles Terry, *Sakuma Shōzan and his Seiken-roku* (Master's thesis, Columbia University, 1951).

tion of Japanese life and thought. Just as the automobiles and petro-chemical refinery complexes imported from (or at least imitated from) the West pollute the Japanese atmosphere, so the ideas and academic approaches of the West pollute the Japanese mind. Unhealthy, over-heated, stuffy Western-style rooms and buildings have replaced the spacious, well-ventilated, aesthetic dwellings of Japan's past. Bodies confined in the tight clothing and pinching shoes of the West lose their natural grace and suppleness. Minds raised in constant confrontation with imported ideas and forced from an early age into repeated contact with foreign languages lose their freshness and have their limpid bloom destroyed.

Contact with reality inevitably destroys the experience of mysticism; contact with the West exposes the Japanese language to a fatal infection, whether the contact is firsthand or only secondhand, through the reading of translations. In one of the most obscure items in the entire sociolinguistic literature, Miura Tsutomu writes about the role of translations in the following words:

> Translation is not only the work of rendering foreign languages into Japanese. It also plays a social role. It exerts an influence upon the linguistic expression of the reader. Through transla-tions, the habits of linguistic expression in foreign languages carry over into the expression of Japanese. When articles in foreign languages are written with many citations of sources, even down to such silly things as the didacticism of personal idols, this begins to infect [densen] those who read such things; they take it to be a golden rule, and then they begin to write articles of similar form.[9]

The language can also suffer from contacts of an opposite nature. It was pointed out in Chapter 2 how much difficulty foreigners experi-ence in learning the Japanese language and how unfamiliar they are with the sociocultural values involved. This difficulty and unfamiliarity

---

[9] Miura Tsutomu, *Nihongo wa dō yū gengo ka?* [What kind of language is Jap-anese?] (Tokyo: Kisetsusha, 1971), p. 222. Author's translation. The word *densen* is the usual medical term for "infection," as in *densenbyō,* "infectious disease." When it comes to the citation of sources, to which Miura is so opposed, perhaps his views reflect the attitude so charmingly expressed long ago by Chamberlain, who in discussing traditional Japanese poetry remarked, "plagiarism [is] accounted no crime, but rather a proof of wide reading and a retentive memory." Basil Hall Chamberlain, *Things Japanese, being notes on various subjects connected with Japan, for the use of travelers and others* (1904; reprint ed. under title *Japanese Things,* Tokyo: Charles E. Tuttle Co., 1974), p. 379.

are more than once suspected, in the sociolinguistic literature, of backing up in the drains and poisoning the sources in a kind of reverse action of linguistic retaliation. The difficulties that foreigners have with the language are so great that, when Japanese help foreigners learn the language, the Japanese run the risk of contaminating the language themselves simply because of their well-meaning efforts to overcome the foreigners' problems. In his book on the language, Suzuki Takao mentions the symptoms and the cause of this occurrence:

> When a Japanese is teaching Japanese to a foreigner, because the person to whom he is teaching it will use broken Japanese, the Japanese person soon finds himself caught up in this, so that often, when he stops to notice, he himself is speaking broken Japanese. What has happened in such a case is that the incorrect Japanese of the person to whom he is speaking has managed to destroy the psychological stability of the Japanese himself.[10]

It was suggested above that the short poetic forms of traditional Japanese literature, particularly the *haiku*, might very well be viewed as metaphors for the transient nature of the mystical experience of the language itself. From this we might also reasonably expect that it would be all but impossible to carry out this segment of the mystical experience in a foreign location, and the correctness of this prediction turns out to be surprisingly easy to document. Uemura Sengyo, editor of a prominent *haiku* journal, reported to the readers of the *Mainichi Shinbun* (Mainichi newspaper) on his difficulties in this connection in an article entitled "Japanese Language Runs Wild." Under the subhead "Difficulties of Writing *haiku* in Foreign Countries," he writes as follows:

> I had often heard tales of how difficult it is to compose *haiku* when one is in a foreign country . . . but what I actually learned firsthand on my recent trip to Europe was that I personally ran up against a thick wall even different from what I had been led to expect from the stories I had heard earlier about this problem. . . . This wall that I ran directly into had to do with the fact that when I was in Europe, and using that language they have over there [*achira no kotoba*] every day, I found that when I tried to use Japanese and write a *haiku*, what do you suppose happened? I myself was startled to find that my own Japanese language had be-

---

[10] Suzuki, *Tozasareta gengo*, p. 187. Author's translation.

67

gun to show signs of becoming disordered, or of what one might call "foreign-language-style craziness" [*acharagoshiki na kurui*]. I was startled to find that my Japanese language as Japanese had lost its potency; and this was not only for writing *haiku*, but even in using Japanese for conversation with other Japanese. . . . In Europe, I only traveled a short time; . . . nevertheless, when you live in a foreign country, your Japanese language begins to run wild. For conversation, English will get you by anywhere. My own English conversation is a rather bogus thing; I just line up nouns, and here and there insert a modifier, nothing more than that. But even so, when I tried to switch back to Japanese and write a *haiku*, I found that the balance [*baransu*] of my Japanese had collapsed. All I could bring off was a simple reportage of events in 5-7-5 syllables, with no savor of a poem about it at all. Truly, Japanese is a mysterious thing [*fushigi na mono*].[11]

Somewhat less elevated, but equally significant, reactions to the role of the West as the ultimate linguistic corrupter are found in two letters, translated from their originals in the *Asahi Shinbun* and printed in the *Asahi Evening News*. They both appeared on the same day.[12]

The first letter, which is headlined "Japanese Names for Promenades," is by Hoseki Matsushima, a public employee from Tokyo:

> I am all for the Metropolitan Police Department's (MPD) plan to start "lunchtime promenades" at 23 spots in Tokyo on October 1 banning automobiles for one hour during lunchtime.
>
> It is reported, however, that MPD will give such promenades nicknames that one may find in some foreign countries. For instance, it plans to call a students' quarter "Young Avenue," a shopping center "Mrs Street" and a business center "Restway."
>
> I imagine the MPD is probably considering providing Japanese people with an international view of things through such names. But I do not think that the blind imitation of foreign names will be of any help to nurture international minds.
>
> There must be beautiful words in the Japanese language that are suitable for nicknames of Japanese streets. I think the only way to enhance the value of the nation in an international society is to respect our own language.

---

[11] *Mainichi Shinbun* [Mainichi newspaper], July 3, 1971. Author's translation.
[12] *Asahi Evening News*, September 29, 1974.

The second letter, which is headlined "Value, Love Our Language," is by Tamiko Nitta, a Yokohama housewife:

> I cannot understand why so many English words are used blindly in TV commercials.
>
> Producers may be trying to make their commercials appear smart. But I don't think it is necessary to use English words in advertisements aimed at Japanese people.
>
> I cannot think of any other country where propaganda for the native people is in a foreign language.
>
> Are commercial producers and advertisers kindly offering us opportunities to practice English?
>
> An American who lives in my neighborhood said to me: "Although they sound like our language, I cannot understand what they mean. Why don't they speak Japanese?"
>
> I know an exotic and new feeling is an important element for commercials, but we should value and love our own language.

The foreign corrupter, in the person of the Westerner and his language, has entered the scene, and nothing will ever be the same again. Various remedies can and will be suggested, but they are almost by definition limited to those of a purely negative cast. Few suggestions differ from the housewife's plea for value and love of the language. Scholars may make somewhat more elegant suggestions. For example, Watanabe Shōichi concluded: "I am convinced that by reexamining the essential qualities of the Yamato language, we will be able to acquire a new insight into the crux of the problems confronting us today in the field of national and foreign language education."[13] But the difference between the two approaches—popular and scholarly—is more apparent than real. Whatever the approach, the issue remains unchanged: the West must be kept out, even if this increasingly seems to be impossible. To solve more difficult present problems, we must go further and further back into the past, even though the further back we go, the less there is to work with. But whatever disadvantages there may be in this process, there is always the major advantage that the further back we go into Japanese cultural and social life, the fewer foreigners there are to be reckoned with—until we approach the ideal Eden of Ōno's preliterate Japan, where they are totally absent.

---

[13] Watanabe Shōichi, "On the Japanese Language," *Japan Echo*, vol. 1, no. 2 (Winter 1974), p. 20.

It remains for us to explore in somewhat more detail a number of the implications inherent in the confrontation between the Japanese language and foreign languages, most especially the problems that arise when non-Japanese foreigners learn and use the language in Japan. But before we can explore those important aspects of the overall question of contemporary sociolinguistic responses to Japanese in Japan, a brief survey of James's fourth mark of mysticism must take priority. Information from the sociolinguistic literature concerning the passivity of the Japanese in relation to their language will then provide an easy transition into the question of the implications of the use of Japanese by non-Japanese.

# 6

# Identification of the Race
# and the Language

William James's fourth mark of mysticism and its ecstatic experiences is that of being passive. Identifying the contemporary Japanese sociolinguistic correlate of this mark in the literature presents no difficulty. Japan itself, viewed as a national and racial entity but without any political overtones, is quite clearly the superior power by which the subject of the mystical experience—the Japanese speaker and user of the language—feels himself to be grasped and held and before whose overwhelming strength his own will finds itself relaxing into a state of more or less total abeyance.

To speak and to use the Japanese language is to be a Japanese; to be a Japanese is to speak and to use the Japanese language. So long as each of these two balanced assumptions is maintained, they reinforce each other; but if either of them is disturbed in the slightest, both collapse. Here we are particularly concerned with a number of the different varieties of evidence available for the nature and causation of such collapses and the disturbances that they set off within the socio-cultural structuring of modern Japan. Since the premises involved are essentially, indeed exclusively, racial in nature, most of these disturbances arise when foreigners enter upon the sociolinguistic scene in one fashion or another. The superior power that overwhelmingly grasps a Japanese in his typical involvement with the mystical experience of his own language is generally identified in the literature with his own racial identity. Disturbances in the given patterns threaten to challenge the validity of that racial identification, and hence they often lead to surprisingly serious consequences, as Suzuki Takao details:

> To a Japanese, the existence of the Japanese language as his national tongue is a self-evident fact. In the same way that we

71

are unconscious of the existence of the air we breathe in our daily lives, so also for the Japanese there is no necessity for being conscious of the existence of the Japanese language. . . . In countries other than Japan, human beings are in a very dynamic [*dainamikku*], a very tense relationship with their language, particularly with their native language. If they let up for even an instant on their efforts not to be separated from it, their own language will be taken from them. When we compare this kind of relationship between a racial group [*minzoku*] and a language with the relationship existing between the Japanese people and the Japanese language, we can only reflect upon what a calm, relaxed situation there is in Japan. Not only do the Japanese totally lack any feeling that if they themselves do not protect their language, if they themselves do not nurture it, it will disappear—quite to the contrary, they end up complaining that Japanese is impracticable, and that it is difficult; they complain that it lacks internationalism, and that it is backward; and finally, in the most extreme cases, one finds the situation where even Ministers of Education and celebrated novelists suggest that it would be better to replace it with a more practical, more rational language— if such could be found! . . . In Japan, we feel that this nation [*kuni*] known as "Japan" is, above everything else, utterly safe and secure; and a part of this concept of security is the language itself, which exists in the nation, where it is both a method of and a tool for daily life. This is why the idea keeps coming up of perhaps changing it for something else, if there is anything better to be found. When we view it in this manner, we can only conclude that the Japanese are not attached to their language by the force of their own wills, but that they merely encounter it as a part of their natural environment. Language, to the Japanese, may be compared to something having the nature of water. We know that water fills every part of a round vessel; but when the vessel is smashed, the water scatters everywhere. The nature [*sugata*] of Japanese today is such that it is a by-product of the natural environment of the nation known as "Japan," and of the human circumstances in that nation. When these change, the Japanese language also quickly changes together with them.[1]

Not everything that Suzuki has to say here is easy to follow, although it has been translated as literally as possible. But enough of his argument survives our reading to make it quite clear that he is talking

---

[1] Suzuki, *Tozasareta gengo*, pp. 194-196. Author's translation.

about the racial correlates of the sociolinguistic approach of the contemporary Japanese intellectual toward the language. Enough is also clear in his analysis so that there can be no mistaking the essentially racial approach of this part of his discussion.

## Linguistic Homogeneity

Suzuki's vague reference to "countries other than Japan" and to the supposed "tense relationship" of their peoples with their languages is amplified elsewhere in his book by short discussions of sociopolitical disputes involving national languages against minor local varieties of speech—for example, linguistic disputes in Belgium. He takes the position that in this respect the Japanese language in Japan is in a uniquely favorable situation, since the country has only one national language and no contenders for its role. The regional dialects have long since lost the battle against the Tokyo variety of the language; hence there is an apparent justification for Suzuki's generalizations in this area.

With the return of Okinawa to Japanese sovereignty, however, this situation of linguistic homogeneity has been seriously upset. Although Suzuki wrote this passage in 1975, he would appear to be writing in the more distant past and thinking about the past. Like so many Japanese intellectuals who were in the forefront of the movement demanding the return of Okinawa to Japanese control, now that Okinawa is once more a part of Japan, he appears to be able quite conveniently to forget that the island exists, that it is a part of Japan, and that its inhabitants do not all speak the Japanese language. They speak Okinawan, a language genetically related to Japanese but mutually unintelligible with it. Confrontations can and do now occur between Japanese citizens who speak different languages. Such an incident occurred just three months before Okinawa reverted to Japanese sovereignty. It received the following coverage and comment in a column in the *Yomiuri Shinbun* [Yomiuri newspaper]:

> The Tokyo District Court was thrown into confusion on February 6 when three Okinawans being tried for setting off firecrackers in the Diet Building last October spoke in "Uchinaguchi" (the Okinawa dialect) when answering the judge's questions.
> "Speak Japanese when you are in court," the judge said. "Uchinaya Nihonyagaya (Is Okinawa Japan?)" the defendants retorted.

The defense counsel said that two of the defendants could not speak Japanese very well, and asked the judge to get an interpreter for them.

The judge refused to grant the request. He said, "I want the defendants to speak in a language that everybody understands. What we call Japanese in court is standard Japanese, which is commonly spoken in Japan. I think the defendants can speak Japanese. . . ."

What motivated the Okinawan defendants to speak the Okinawan dialect in court? This is the question that must be asked and answered.

After Okinawa was annexed to Japan in the early Meiji Era, the Japanese Government forced Okinawans to speak standard Japanese. This historical fact still hangs implicitly over Okinawa.

Perhaps it is this that led the Okinawan defendants to speak Uchinaguchi (the Okinawan dialect), instead of Yamatoguchi (Japanese), in court.

Perhaps they think Japan is going to rule Okinawa again.

Old people in Okinawa often use the expression Ikutoubanushinasaki, which means "the human touch contained in spoken language."

Many Uchinanchu (Okinawans) think that Yamatoguchi (Japanese), spoken by Yamatonchu (Japanese), lacks the human touch, though it sounds good.

All the same, we think Okinawans ought to speak in Japanese when answering the judge's questions in court.

There may well be Ikutoubanushinasaki in standard Japanese, too.[2]

Okinawa is now both in fact and in law a part of Japan again. Its non-Japanese speakers are, presumably, all busy speaking the same Japanese language that the Japanese in Japan take as equivalent to "the air we breathe." Japan's linguistic homogeneity, like any other kind of overriding social uniformity, will be bought at the price of stamping out, or at least driving underground, all nonconformist patterns, whether they are the local nonstandard dialects of the home islands or independent linguistic entities such as the Okinawan language.[3]

---

[2] *Daily Yomiuri*, February 26, 1972; the article originally appeared in Japanese, under the head *Henshū techō*, in the *Yomiuri Shinbun*.

[3] The use of the term *Okinawa dialect*, as in the *Yomiuri* excerpts above, is yet another example of semantic slanting of the issues involved. By any usual linguistic definition and terminology, Okinawan is a language, genetically related to home-island Japanese, to be sure, but by no possible stretch of linguistic usage to be considered one of its dialects.

One even looks in vain for much evidence concerning the "calm, relaxed situation" that Suzuki supposes to have resulted from the implementation of this rigid linguistic homogeneity with respect to the nonstandard dialects of the home islands themselves. The following letter to the *Asahi Evening News* from a high school student in Sendai is headlined "Preserve Local Dialects":

> When I read the vivid dialog of the Sendai dialect in Hisashi Inoue's novel, "Aoba Shigereru" (Leaves grow thick), I envied the hero and the characters speaking the dialect.
>
> Students in Sendai seem to have ceased to speak the dialect recently.
>
> I doubt if I can find any students who speak the Sendai dialect perfectly in my school.
>
> I think this tendency is not limited to students in Sendai. . . .
>
> Are there only a few people remaining who speak a dialect freely? I am very surprised at the great impact of TV culture—which is influencing people to lose the accent of their regions.
>
> Although language teachers say dialects should be corrected, I miss dialects very much.
>
> I am attracted by dialects because they impart a warm feeling of each region where they are spoken, which the standard language doesn't have.
>
> Even I, who was born and raised in Sendai, am unable to speak with a Sendai accent before others without picking up courage. I am very sad about this.[4]

This poignant letter is perhaps testimony to a calm, relaxed attitude, but it is more likely a description of sociolinguistic defeat.

---

[4] *Asahi Evening News*, September 29, 1974.

# 7

# Reactions to Foreigners' Speaking
# the Language

Any facet of Japanese life or culture is thrown into sharp relief when it is brought into direct confrontation with a similar or parallel foreign phenomenon. This contrast is most striking when the Japanese language and its speakers come into confrontation with foreign languages, particularly English and its speakers; but in this chapter we will address ourselves to the equally knotty if less obvious question of the sociolinguistic reaction of contemporary Japanese to the use of their own language by foreigners.

That the Japanese have rather unexpected, and at times rather strange, reactions to the spectacle of foreigners learning, using, and above all speaking the Japanese language has been more than adequately documented in the literature at least since the first part of the present century. Basil Hall Chamberlain (1850–1935), a pioneer foreign student of the Japanese language and a trenchant observer of things Japanese, put it in the following way: "seeing that you speak Japanese, they will wag their heads and smile condescendingly, and admit to each other that you are really quite intelligent—much as we might do in the presence of the learned pig or an ape of somewhat unusual attainments."[1]

Few of us who have learned Japanese and who have lived and worked in modern Japan using the language in our daily activities would wish to suggest that Chamberlain's seven-decade-old description requires updating or revision in any important way. Effective employment of the Japanese language in Japan today by a person who is not

---

[1] Chamberlain, *Things Japanese*, p. 382.

of Japanese racial origin still elicits the same reactions that the English traveler and scholar described so well. Here we must address ourselves to the question that has occurred to everyone who, for the simple reason of his command of the Japanese language, has been compared to "the learned pig or an ape of somewhat unusual accomplishments." The question is, in a word, why?

### The Law of Inverse Returns

Every non-Japanese who becames involved in learning the Japanese language must contend with a facet of sociolinguistic behavior that can be called the law of inverse returns. This law holds that the better you get at the language, the less credit you are given for your accomplishments; the more fluently you speak it, the less your hard-won skills will do for you in the way of making friends and favorably impressing people; but by the same token the less you can do with the language, the more you will be praised and encouraged by Japanese society in general and your friends in particular.

It would appear that this curious law of inverse returns applies only to Europeans and Americans, to use the delicate Japanese euphemism for what we equally delicately term Caucasians—that is, whites. Koreans, Chinese, Southeast Asians, even Indians from India are exempt from its curiously involute provisions.[2] Nonwhites are expected to know Japanese if they live or work in Japan for extended periods, and it is surely no accident that for several decades following World War II the only Japanese-language training program provided for non-Japanese by the Japanese government was a small language school that specialized exclusively in teaching the language to Southeast Asians and other nonwhites.

Any sociolinguistic phenomenon as baffling as this law of inverse returns tempts one to analyze its origins. Interesting and significant factors must surely lie behind the evolution of any set of behavior patterns as rigidly, and as abstractly, structured as these. The white foreigner who learns a few words of the Japanese language may easily be forgiven for gaining the impression that he has mastered the entire

---

[2] Surprisingly explicit references to what he very clearly terms "the difference between the attitude of Japanese toward whites speaking Japanese and nonwhites speaking Japanese" are made in Suzuki, *Tozasareta gengo*, p. 180.

language in a matter of minutes.[3] He has only to say a few everyday greetings in anything approaching recognizable pronunciation to be told that he "speaks Japanese better than we do ourselves." Let him generate a complete sentence and his friends and drinking companions will all but fall from their barstools in unabashed admiration for his incredible linguistic gifts. Such successes naturally tempt anyone to further experiments and, since one learns a foreign language by actually using it, in the natural course of events the foreigner in Japan does in most cases get better and better at the language.

It is when he really begins making progress in his control of the spoken language that he first notices his friends' reactions cooling down. He now hears less and less about how "skillful" (*jōzu*) he is in Japanese. He might wonder if he is even communicating, although it should be obvious from the extralinguistic evidence available to him that he is (for example, the telephoned order for *sushi* is delivered, questions he asks on the street for information are answered, and so on). The moment of truth will come when he happens to be in a position to overhear a relative newcomer to the country told, "How skillful you are with Japanese; you speak better than we do ourselves." The newcomer receives the treatment that he has now outgrown. He can hear for himself how halting and stumbling the newcomer's Japanese really is, and he can hear his Japanese friends on every side telling each other how well the newcomer speaks. Obviously there is something important behind all this.

### Suzuki's Documentation of the Law

Although Suzuki Takao does not formulate the law of inverse returns as such, he does document its operation in modern Japanese society in elaborate detail, and he attempts an analysis that will serve us well in our investigation here. At the outset, it should be made clear how important his documentation is; this is because it is extremely important to have the workings of this curious law fully established by competent Japanese observers, hence removing any suspicion that the entire phenomenon is nothing more than the paranoiac fantasy of oversensitive

---

[3] The impression is reflected in such journalistic efforts as Samuel Greenburg, "I Can Teach You All the Japanese You'll Ever Need to Know," *New York Times*, January 10, 1971.

foreigners. It is emphatically not anything of the sort. It is a significant facet of modern Japanese sociolinguistic behavior, and it is important to have the documentation that Suzuki provides so that we may establish its operation without any questions being raised concerning the accuracy of our own personal observations.

Suzuki presents four documents, reprinting selections from published accounts in which foreigners long resident in Japan and fluent in the language have described their experiences speaking the language. Implicit in his selection of each of these documents is his claim that it embodies a facet of contemporary sociolinguistic behavior that he has himself witnessed and to which he would like to draw attention.

In the first document, Wilhelm Grootaers, a Belgian missionary-scholar who has resided in Japan for many years, is directed to the wrong ticket window when he tries to buy a ticket for a program of Japanese-language comic sketches at a theater. Even though he asks in Japanese for the correct ticket, the girl behind the box office window insists on selling him a ticket for the European movie playing elsewhere in the same theater complex, assuming that she knows better than the Japanese-speaking Caucasian what he really wants to see. She simply cannot believe that he would wish to purchase a ticket that will admit him to a program of comic sketches performed in the Japanese language, even though he says to her quite clearly in Japanese that that is precisely what he wishes to do. Then, when he finally has managed to get into the program of comic sketches and has been sitting there for some three-and-a-half hours laughing at all the Japanese-language jokes and applauding the outrageous Japanese-language puns and sallies, a Japanese gentleman sitting next to him says in English, "Excuse me," when he finds it necessary to disturb Grootaers in order to leave early. Might not someone who has been sitting there that long and so obviously enjoying the highly verbal humor of the performers be assumed to understand also the Japanese for "Excuse me"? Not in Japan, and not if the person in question is a Caucasian foreigner.

In the second of Suzuki's documents, a British scholar of Japanese literature comments in detail on how often he has been told that "the better you speak Japanese, the worse impression we Japanese have of you."

In the third document, Donald Keene reacts to the people who, after telling him how much they admire his translations into English from classical Japanese literature, apologize for handing him their name-cards if the cards do not have their names printed in romanization along with the usual Chinese characters. Might not someone who can obviously read the entire range of classical Japanese literature be expected to be able to read a namecard at least as well as most Japanese can? Not in Japan, and not if the subject is a Caucasian foreigner.

Finally, a British Broadcasting Company executive, a longtime resident in Japan, describes a truly bewildering experience involving a conversation with the Japanese receptionist of a large Tokyo company. In reply to his carefully repeated, accurately pronounced, and completely grammatical inquiries in Japanese about an appointment with her employer, the receptionist simply kept repeating over and over in her all but unintelligible English, "Excuse me, I am sorry, I do not understand."

To each of these documents Suzuki adds explanations for the Japanese readers of his book concerning the individuals involved. He testifies that the foreigners in question in each case really do know the language and really do speak quite fluent and completely intelligible Japanese. Then he addresses himself to the question of why these things happen:

> I have cited these four documents by these four foreigners because, despite the fact that they somewhat overlap one another in content, each of these documents nevertheless provides excellent insights into the question of just how the average Japanese individual [*ippan no Nihonjin*] really feels about his own language. Let me sum up the important points that the testimony of each of these four documents has in common. First I would note the fact that most Japanese still have not yet freed themselves from their "fear of foreigners" [he explains his Japanese term *gaijin kyōfushō* for this with "xenophobia" as a gloss in romanization immediately following the Sino-Japanese word]. . . . Despite the fact that every year more than two million Japanese tourists go abroad, and also despite the fact that even here in Japan the opportunities for coming into contact with foreigners are immeasurably more numerous than in the past, I must conclude that psychologically we Japanese are still by no means liberated from our sense of fear and our feelings of terror concerning contacts with foreigners. It would not do to be misunderstood in the matter of using such terms as *fear* or *terror*, which have nuances that might be misleading in this context. Perhaps it would be better simply to call what we are talking about "a sense of psychological unrest." When we encounter a foreigner,

81

our psychological security disintegrates. Our hearts begin to flutter; normal cognitive processes cease; and we are unable to pursue balanced activities. . . . We experience a kind of "stage fright" when we encounter foreigners. Then, when under these circumstances someone replies in his own halting English to the perfectly fluent Japanese-language question of some foreigner, and perhaps even asks him, in bad English, "Do you speak Japanese?" we must conclude that such a person has clearly demonstrated that he is not operating in a normal psychological state.[4]

## Suzuki's Analysis

Suzuki's first concrete proposal for the analysis of this phenomenon has to do with the question of violating sociolinguistic territorial integrity. Such violation, as he puts it, is well known to cause severe reactions and to bring about extreme psychological disturbances in the case of all the higher animals: why should the sociolinguistic situation in Japan be any exception? The Japanese person speaking Japanese in Japan is on his home sociolinguistic territory par excellence, and he is operating there with maximal effectiveness. A foreigner speaking Japanese invades this territory at his own risk. If he speaks halting Japanese, he may invade this sociolinguistic territory with relative impunity. He will even be praised and flattered for his few words of Japanese simply because his command of the language is obviously so imperfect that he cannot be considered a serious contender for the territory. His territorial violation is real enough, but he is obviously not worth worrying about.

This breaks down rapidly, in direct proportion to the extent to which the foreigner becomes fluent in the language. The outsider who violates territorial integrity may no longer be ignored, or condoned, or even rewarded with meaningless praise from the moment when he gives evidence that his invasion is more than a casual event or a careless accident. Genuine fluency in Japanese by foreigners living and working in Japan provides overt evidence of large-scale, long-lasting, and extremely serious invasion of sociolinguistic territorial interests that are to be defended. To speak Japanese with a foreigner is to admit defeat in this battle over territorial invasion. The receptionist who chose to repeat "I do not understand" in English over and over in response to

---

[4] Suzuki, *Tozasareta gengo*, pp. 174-175. Author's translation.

the BBC executive's completely understandable Japanese inquiry was defending her own and her employer's sociolinguistic territorial integrity in the only way possible for her to do so—by pretending that the invasion had not actually taken place at all, in the hope that it would, if ignored long enough and pointedly enough, simply go away. Of course, her approach to the problem also made it impossible for her employer to keep his appointment to see the Englishman in question. Despite that, she was still, in a very real sense, guarding his territorial integrity.

Suzuki's second point is a bit more convoluted and a little less easy to explain, but it is important to his analysis. He holds that these four documents together testify to the strength of the belief, which he claims is generally held among Japanese, that "foreigners ought not, properly, to understand Japanese at all" (*gaikokujin ni wa Nihongo ga wakaru hazu ga nai*). For all the difficulties of translation it poses, this statement is completely normal Japanese and quite a usual way of saying what he is trying to say. The difficult term to translate is the noun *hazu*. The word has semantic undertones of normality, regularity, and natural order—nuances that even extend, depending upon the context, into the spheres of ethical and moral conduct.[5] It is this *hazu*—this natural expectation of ethical, moral normality and regularity, this standard of natural order—that is violated when foreigners give evidence that they understand Japanese by using it and speaking it. When foreigners do use the language, something is ethically and morally out of joint somewhere in the natural order of the universe, and caution is urged on the part of all.

It would be somewhat unfair to Suzuki's analysis to underestimate either the importance of this second point or the seriousness with which he is making it simply because what he has to say is cloaked so deeply in what might be termed the "nontechnical technical language" of modern Japanese intellectual dialectic. Such turns of expression as the vague phrase *hazu ga nai* (where in addition to the *hazu*, already discussed, the *ga nai* is simply the subject marker followed by the negative copula "is not") are perfectly acceptable Japanese usage in the context

---

[5] The extension of sociolinguistic concerns into the area of ethics and morality is yet another aspect of the problem to which no attention has been devoted in the present monograph, primarily out of considerations of space. In Japan such concerns are deeply involved with longstanding Confucian concepts of the ethical-moral nature of the speech act and with important ideas ultimately deriving from neo-Confucian cosmological speculation.

of such discussions. They are widely tolerated by Japanese intellectuals for employment as key steps in the development of their argumentation on a wide variety of topics, language and sociolinguistic behavior included. If we happen to find such phrases bewilderingly abstract, difficult to pin down semantically, and prone to crumble into the ashes of meaninglessness at the merest gesture on our part toward definition or clarification, these are problems involved with our understanding of the Japanese language and of the Japanese mentality that finds its expression in that language. They are hardly problems of proper concern for the Japanese themselves. But that does not mean that the problems examined in such vague passages are any less real.

Suzuki makes it clear that for him at least the mastery and utilization of the Japanese language by foreigners implies an upset of the natural order of things, and also that these implications of upset carry strong secondary adumbrations of something unnatural, even at times of unethical and immoral activities. These are things that can only, in the normal course of events, be expected to result in escalating social disorder and sociolinguistic disaster. A foreigner speaking Japanese amounts to the public performance of an unnatural act. Such flouting of the natural order (here to be understood in general and historical Confucian terms, with *nature* as a synonym for morality and ethical culture) can only result in natural retribution. Hence, any sensible person shuns direct contact with such dangerous episodes. Only the fool openly challenges nature to take its revenge.

Suzuki's closing comments on this subject are so illuminating that they deserve translation and citation at some length:

> Thus we might well ask ourselves, how has it come about that we Japanese, when confronted by a foreigner, and with him speaking Japanese to us, take attitudes such as those [described above] which the foreigner must find incomprehensible from his point of view, as well as being for him disagreeable in the extreme? How have we come to have such prejudices? . . . Not only is our country a completely isolated island, with no borders directly touching upon any other foreign country (compare this with France, which has boundaries with six countries), but we do not have any large numbers of different races within our nation. Moreover, . . . historically we have never had a direct invasion by foreigners. Very few of us have friends or acquaintances who are foreigners; and it is all but impossible to find a Japanese today who has any foreigners numbered among his immediate relatives, much less

among his distant ancestors. All this is completely different in the case of the Americans, of course, but it is also different with the major races of Europe and Asia. There we find many persons who have foreigners for grandfathers and grandmothers. The English royal family is related by marriage to royal and noble houses of almost every nation in Europe. When we view the problem in this fashion, we will understand that the pathological fear of foreigners that we Japanese have is a deeply rooted racial-cultural characteristic [*ne no fukai minzoku bunkateki na tokushitsu*], something too deeply rooted to disappear overnight. . . . The conviction that foreigners ought not, properly, to understand [*wakaru hazu ga nai*] the Japanese language is of course not without its own connection to the point just made. If there were more contacts between Japanese and persons from other countries, the number of foreigners using Japanese would naturally increase; in that case, the sight of a foreigner speaking Japanese would gradually become less unusual, and one would expect that the resulting feeling of unnatural behavior on our part would in such cases gradually diminish.[6] However, as of the present time, a foreigner who can speak Japanese well is an exceptional case, and for that very reason [*sore dake ni*] those few who do are continually insulted by being treated like "talking dogs."[7]

Suzuki touches many bases in this passage. He is correct enough about the origins of the House of Windsor, and he has a good grasp of the geography of France. Otherwise, very little can be said for his historical assumptions that underlie this passage, particularly his assumption of a monoracial origin for all Japanese. His facts, in other words, are almost completely inaccurate, but his point that the diverse phenomena of sociolinguistic behavior involved in the Japanese reaction to the use of the Japanese language by foreigners relate ultimately to the essential racial orientation of modern Japanese culture is of tremendous value and profound interest for our study. If Suzuki's

---

[6] The key word here probably is "gradually." Even at the November 1972 International Conference on Japanese Studies sponsored in Kyoto by the Japanese PEN Club, nothing provided as much surprise for the Japanese press and other media in general than the spectacle of foreigners talking Japanese—not only to Japanese but, on occasion, to each other! See, for example, John McCaleb, "Foreign Scholars Amaze Delegates with Fluency in Japanese," *Daily Yomiuri*, November 30, 1972.

[7] Suzuki, *Tozasareta gengo*, pp. 176-177. Author's translation.

statement is less an exposition of his analysis than it is a self-demonstration of his thesis, it is only all the more valuable on this very account.

The key term in Suzuki's presentation is *minzoku bunkateki na tokushitsu* ("racial-cultural characteristic"). This is another of the elusive phrases so dear to the written style of modern Japanese scholarship and so resistant to correct translation and explanation. It is not that they are particularly complex or profound but that they are generally centered upon specious abstractions—in this case, the noun *tokushitsu*. In a context such as this, *tokushitsu* implies that the features or characteristics to which it has reference are not only special and distinctive but also solely and uniquely Japanese. Further, it clearly suggests that these characteristics or features are of an order of refinement and delicacy not to be known or identified *outside the context of Japanese culture.*[8] When this has been made clear, we begin to understand more of the essential thrust of Suzuki's passage.

The progression of ideas by means of which Suzuki arrives at this formulation confronts us with one fascinating insight after another into the thinking of many modern Japanese intellectuals on these questions. The ideas are all the more striking in this case because Suzuki is a widely traveled, widely experienced scholar, a person specializing in foreign-language study and its problems, and a person who surely cannot be accused of lacking firsthand familiarity with foreign countries or world history and geography. But it is evident from this passage that, for him, Japan is still very much an island, and a closed-country island at that, for all the world as if Commodore Perry had never landed and the treaty ports had never been forced open. Modern transportation facilities might just as well not exist. Korea, Guam, and Hawaii are crowded almost all the year around with Japanese tourists, but this does not count. Totally overlooked are the well-documented continental blood-line connections of the Japanese imperial family, not to mention almost every other important

---

[8] The word *tokushitsu* appears, correctly enough, in bilingual dictionaries translated as "special characteristic, character, feature; distinctive feature," and these glosses are sufficient for an understanding of the surface meaning of the word. What they do not make clear, however, is the existence of another level of connotations within the deep structure of the language, connotations that may best be approximated with the translation "unique." The other words in the phrase are more straightforward: *minzoku* is "race" and *bunkateki* is "cultural." In this expression both these words are linked syntactically to the noun *tokushitsu* by the copula surrogate *na*.

family of the Old Japanese period. Disregarded is all the evidence of continental elements in the formation of the early Japanese state and nation, not to mention the massive Allied occupation of the country following Japan's defeat in World War II. For Suzuki, history has stood still, and most of it has simply not happened.

What Suzuki has to say in this passage concerning the monolithic, isolated, racially pure origins of Japanese life and society are directly and simply contradicted by everything that is known of the actual history of the development of these institutions. Historically, the Japanese islands have been the end, the point of no return, on a route for multiple movements and population shifts of all varieties, if not for proper invasions. The Japanese islands have always been the last landing point for those fleeing the continent of Asia for one reason or another and, once these fugitives got to Japan, they stayed there, if only for the simple geographical fact that there was no place further for them to go.

Even the Japanese myth itself preserves rich evidence for the early complexity of the Japanese race and Japanese cultural life and for the diverse strands out of which both were woven in the first centuries of our era. Japan's physical separation from the Korean peninsula has never been sufficiently great to ensure, much less permit, genuine isolation anything like the splendid solitude that Suzuki conjures up.[9] Even the closed-country policies of the Tokugawa period (which above everything else is what Suzuki has in mind here, extending it in his imagination to the entire range of Japanese history) were adopted not so much to prevent foreign intercourse as to regulate it and to bring an end to the already major inroads that the Portuguese and Spanish merchants and missionaries had made into the country. The policy was one of expulsion, but for expulsion there must first be something to expel. Thus, without further belaboring the issue, Suzuki's facts do not hold up under scrutiny. But his zeroing in on the racial and cultural nature of the question of the use of Japanese by foreigners is what interests us, and the question is thrown into sharper relief by the gaps in his data.

---

[9] See Gari Ledyard, "Galloping Along with the Horseriders: Looking for the Founders of Japan," *Journal of Japanese Studies*, vol. 1 (1975), pp. 217-254, for a good presentation of what is now understood by scholars concerning the early Japanese-Korean relationship, but with the serious drawback that it is both unreliable and uninformed concerning the linguistic details of the issue.

One further passage from Suzuki may help to establish his position on these questions:

> The Japanese language is firmly bound up with this land "Japan," and it forms a common entity with the Japanese race and with Japanese culture. In my view, the way in which the Japanese think about their own language displays extremely strong characteristics of what might very well be termed *person-orientation*. This person-orientation is a concept that contrasts with *location-orientation*, and it is not unrelated to the standards that are applied in determining the legal nationality of a newborn child. There can be no doubt that we Japanese, who are born as the children of parents both of whom are Japanese, are automatically Japanese. This way of thinking is the most natural for Japanese; and even if they should have a child while residing abroad, it is usual for them not even to consider the possibility that any question might ever possibly arise concerning that child's nationality. But for example, in such countries as the United States, what determines a newborn child's nationality is not the nationality of its parents, but the place where it is born. Consequently a child born in the United States of Japanese parents residing there has, in principle, American nationality. But for the Japanese, being a Japanese is in the final analysis a question of blood [*chi no mondai*], not one of law or of regulation.[10]

There is nothing in the above passage, which was published in 1975, that could not have been written in 1942; there is very little in it that could not have been written in 1895. Suzuki provides us with vivid evidence of how little things have changed in this area of sociolinguistic behavior, despite the superficially striking changes that the post-World War II years have visited upon at least the external behavior patterns of Japanese society. The identification of the language with the race is still supreme; violation of one is violation of the other.

Given this impressive evidence that in sociolinguistics, as probably in everything else, the more things change, the more they are the same, one is hard put to select a termination point for these attempts to present and analyze data. The following "document" is a convenient closing for the present study because it brings together a number of questions considered in this chapter. It is a letter from a Tokyo resi-

---

[10] Suzuki, *Tozasareta gengo*, p. 177. Author's translation.

dent that appeared in the *Asahi Evening News* under the headline "Foreigners' Humor in Colloquial Japanese":

> An Argentine, who is here to study Japanese literature and contributes serial articles on "Life in Japan" to the Asahi, wrote recently in his column about the critical response from Japanese readers to his view of the Japanese language. . . .
>
> I am impressed with the Argentine's linguistic ability and think we should do justice to his past efforts. . . . He indeed writes better than the average Japanese.
>
> However, I would like to give him a (perhaps needless) piece of advice, all the more because I highly appreciate his performance. His serial articles make us smile and chuckle. But does he know this smile has some sort of bitterness in it? A wry smile, as you may say. . . .
>
> I earnestly hope he gives serious attention to why the smile had to be wry . . . and this problem is, I think, applicable to almost all foreigners who are proficient in the Japanese language.
>
> Japanese have been criticized as having no Western sense of humor. But this requires a little correction. In fact we have it, but only halfway. We can see Western (including of course the Southern hemisphere) humor, even when applied to the Japanese way of life, so long as it is couched in Western languages; but we cannot bear to see it clothed in our own language. Curiously, the more colloquial the language becomes, the more the humor bites us.
>
> Foreigners well versed in Japanese may not notice it, but we get nervous or sometimes indignant when they speak very colloquially and HUMOROUSLY about things Japanese. Therefore, when you want to communicate with Japanese by means of their language without arousing needless irritation because of your humor, the best way may be not to adopt very fluent colloquialism.[11]

If the author of this letter had been making a conscious attempt to document some of the major sociolinguistic concerns that our study has revealed thus far, he could not have done a better or a more useful job for the purposes of our present inquiry.

---

[11] *Asahi Evening News,* December 12, 1974.

# 8

# Conclusions: The Need for Caution

The Japanese approach their language within a mystical framework supported by a mythical foundation of beliefs about its structure and operation. This places the relationship of the Japanese to their language in a unique setting that affects their social and linguistic reactions to situations involving the language. The importance of this distinctive relationship is especially evident when the language comes into contact with the outside world, either through non-Japanese speaking the language or through translation. Both situations violate the need for exclusiveness and other features essential for the Japanese experience of their language, and both call for the exercise of extreme tact and circumspection.

The data and analysis we have presented also hint at broader strands underlying the Japanese social fabric. Within the Japanese cultural world, incidents cannot be evaluated properly outside of their context; but to consider them within their proper context is difficult because the forces influencing actions are difficult for outsiders to perceive and interpret. Understanding the meaning of an occurrence requires a broad and objective study of the Japanese culture. Cultural concerns, however, are not clearly and unambiguously exhibited, perhaps because their undisputed importance precludes the necessity for display. These concerns differ significantly from those felt in the United States, even if similar underlying forces are at work. For Westerners, sensitivity and caution are mandatory when approaching the Japanese language.

This survey of the popular (and a portion of the scholarly) sociolinguistic literature concerning Japanese clearly indicates that, when we approach closely to the working of the language within the context of the culture, we are by that same token approaching closely to the parameters of a modern myth. This is the myth of the special, unique nature of the Japanese language, the myth of the language as a vehicle for ineffable qualities and quantities that result in a sociolinguistic orientation that almost precisely coordinates with William James's classic definition of a state of mystical experience. It is a myth that generates a mystic approach, and out of this same mystic approach the myth itself in turn grows and is strengthened. The Japanese attitude toward their language cannot be understood apart from the system and apparatus of mysticism that perpetuates it. To approach either the language or the culture in any of their diverse modern manifestations without appreciating this fact is to run the risk of serious sociological disturbances, since one cannot insensitively confront the basis of the mythic belief of an entire culture without arousing hostile reactions on the part of the individuals that belong to that culture. This is why at least some understanding of the mythic dimensions of the sociolinguistic orientation of Japanese in modern Japan is essential for an understanding of any modern Japanese activity or institution. This complex situation alone would be sufficient reason for the exercise of extraordinary caution in all sociolinguistic situations involving the Japanese language, but there are other indications as well of the need for caution.

## Central Role of the Myth

Caution in such encounters is also indicated by the evidence that we have here uncovered for the surprisingly central role that this myth, inseparable from its sustaining fabric of mysticism, plays within modern Japanese life and culture. In modern Japan the technical questions of the Japanese language are not things of interest only to scholars. They are of interest to everyone. It is only the foreign observer of the Japanese scene who has not been fully aware of this fact, largely because until now little if any of the relevant sociolinguistic literature has been available to the non-Japanese reader. Moreover, this literature has not seemed to many Japan specialists in the West particularly relevant to their work of learning more and understanding more about Japan and the Japanese. This unverbalized assumption and the attendant neglect of this area certainly seem to have been both unwarranted and misleading. The sociolinguistic literature, to which the present monograph simply presents an introduction, offers a rare opportunity for the foreign observer to study the Japanese in the process of their almost constant occupation of attempting to understand themselves.

Books that deal with these sociolinguistic questions—generally on a somewhat superficial level—sell in great quantities. In every issue the daily newspapers carry both news and feature articles that in some way or other touch upon these issues; often the notices are in the form of special articles dealing specifically with these questions. Despite their increasing size, Japanese newspapers and popular weekly magazines still operate under severe limitations of space. Every inch of their pages is precious, and they do not devote any of their columns to any topic without good reason and considerable deliberation. The fact that so many news accounts and editorial features dealing with sociolinguistic questions appear in the Japanese press is another excellent indication of the enormous importance of this major modern myth of the language.

We are not dealing with something of exclusive interest to scholars. These sociolinguistic questions are of continuing and undiminished interest to Japanese of all levels of education and apparently on all levels of society. Housewives write letters about them to the newspapers; presidents of major companies contribute features on them to the editorial pages of the same papers; students—that most elastic of all sociological categories in Japanese life—express their continuing concern about these issues in a variety of ways, not the least of which is buying and reading the mountain of publications that appear, both on the popular and on the more specifically scholarly level.

One of the principal functions of a myth is to provide a focus for a social group, a common point about which that group may center its life and work. This focus is immune to the otherwise normal concerns of logic, reason, and common sense, and for that reason it is all the more important and durable. This is the role that the modern myth of the Japanese language in Japan plays so superbly. Differences of opinion are always allowable in matters of detail, and it is the detailed working-out of these allowable differences that accounts for the bulk of the sociolinguistic literature. But there is neither the opportunity nor the need for differences over the basic body of the mythic structure itself: the myth is something that everyone can agree upon, and the mystical structure that perpetuates the myth is an experience in which all members of the society are able to participate equally. When we understand something of these considerations, we begin to understand better why caution is required in any confrontation between this myth and an outsider to the sociolinguistic group.

### Lack of Demythologizers

In modern sociocultural experience, when we locate a myth, we expect, as a matter of course, also to discover the work of demythologizers. The existence of the one almost automatically triggers the evolution of the other. If the modern myth of the Japanese language in Japan is truly special or unique, as the sociolinguistic writers so often claim, it is unique partly in the striking absence of any demythologizing forces within the culture. This is negative evidence, but it still is of tremendous importance for a fuller understanding of the ways in which the Japanese themselves approach the Japanese language. A hundred voices are raised in Japan every day attesting to the durability of the myth and perpetuating its mystical phenomenology, or trappings, but one looks almost in vain in the literature for a single voice arguing against the myth or suggesting that what is important is not the outline of the myth itself but the kernel of truth that it has grown up around. In brief, one looks in vain for the demythologizers in this field. This fact makes it truly a most remarkable, probably a unique, modern myth.

Even more striking is the fact that the very areas within Japanese society where one might normally expect the demythologizers to arise provide instead the most stalwart champions of the myth and its mystic rituals. Considering the nature of the subject matter involved in the myth—in broadest terms, the nature, structure, and history of the Japanese language—one might reasonably expect that the ranks of the demythologizers would be filled by the professional, academic scholars of the structure and history of the Japanese language. But our investigations have shown that just the opposite is true. The scholars professionally concerned with these topics in Japanese academic life are not the demythologizers; they are the principal perpetuators of the myth and the chief practitioners of the mystical cult.

Academic life and university appointments still carry surprising prestige in Japanese life. Newspaper, magazine, and television media ask the opinions of university faculty members on a variety of subjects, much as in other countries popular actors, musicians, and athletes are solicited for their views on issues of the day. By and large, it is academic persons professionally involved with questions of the Japanese language who are queried by the media about these sociolinguistic questions. This might well be an opportune juncture in the system where we would expect a move toward demythologization to emerge, but the fact of the matter is that just the opposite happens. The academic establishment in these fields perpetuates the myth. The extremely minor and elusive moves in the direction of demythologization do not originate within Japanese academia. The tremendous prestige of the Japanese university system is almost totally directed toward the perpetuation of the myth, not toward its overthrow or even its reinvestigation. This is another fact of the modern sociolinguistic situation in Japan that must result in a counsel of caution, if for no other reason than that it is so very unexpected.

## Antiquity and Durability of the Myth

The fact that we have here identified the main outlines of a major modern myth, alive and well within contemporary Japanese sociolinguistic culture, should not trap us into the mistake of thinking that the myth is solely modern. Again, our survey of the literature immediately indicates how and why that is not the case. The myth is modern, to be sure, but that does not by any means indicate that it is of modern origin or contemporary generation. To assume this would be a dangerous oversimplification. Almost every detail of its modern manifestations has deep roots in the mainstream of traditional Japanese culture and thought. The myth is modern in the sense that it is a vigorous component of the modern scene; it is modern in the sense that it is an integral part of the thinking and intellectual equipment of modern Japanese life and culture; but it is not modern in the sense that it is something manufactured in recent times or produced in our day for some particular goal or end. The essential ingredients of the myth have been available within Japanese literary culture since the time of the *Man'yōshū* anthology. The surprising thing about this is probably not the fact that these principal components of the myth are so old, but the fact that they give so little indication of their tremendous antiquity when we view them in their contemporary versions. An excellent case in point is the concept of *koto-dama,* or the spirit of the language, which is a major focal point of the myth and a major ingredient in the mystical conception of the language. We have observed in the writing of Watanabe Shōichi in *Japan Echo* that this concept is as vigorous today as it was well over a thousand years ago in the pages of the first Japanese poetic anthology.

This particular aspect of the question helps illuminate the general thrust and overall outlines of Japanese cultural life since it provides an excellent arena in which to observe the characteristic genius of traditional Japanese culture. This genius is here exemplified in the remarkable ability of the Japanese culture to tolerate diversity without allowing fundamental change and, in the process, to manage the almost unchanged preservation and transmission of sizable portions of its ancient intellectual inheritance from the remote past down to the present day. A large number of essential concepts, ideas, standards, and patterns of behavior have been perpetuated more or less unchanged across the dimension of time, despite the major alterations in more visible aspects of Japanese life.

This, of course, is not to argue for the Western myth of the "unchanging East," much less for the chimera of an "unchanging Japan"; there simply is no such thing. There have indeed been major upheavals in Japan, most particularly with the coming of modernization. Japanese life and culture have been wrenched and racked by one crisis after another. But despite all this change, one may still discern the traces of unaltered and persistent major mythic themes in the culture. The sociolinguistic approach of the Japanese to their language demonstrates great continuity despite the manifold changes that have occurred over the centuries.

From Professor Watanabe back to the ancient poets is a long span of history, one during which Japanese life and culture have sustained every imaginable variety of shock; yet directly across this long span of time we are able to discern an almost unaltered area of mythic concern about the language and an almost unchanged approach of mysticism toward the way in which the language works with respect to the society it serves. Again, the only possible conclusion is a call for great caution. Any cultural element that is this durable clearly represents issues of extraordinary value for the civilization in which it is found, and therefore should be approached by the outsider only after careful study and prolonged and cautious investigation.

# Derivative Myths

Furthermore, the fact that the myth of the Japanese language is a major modern phenomenon does not mean that within this myth there are not many subsidiary or derivative myths. We have explored several of these, particularly those derivative myths that fit in so very well with the classical structuring of the mystical experience as originally sketched by James. It has not been possible to explore all the ramifications of the myth in these pages. But enough has been surveyed to make it clear why the entire subject deserves not only careful study but also the exercise of extreme caution. And lest we fall into the trap of believing that this major myth, with its constellation of derivative myths, is something enjoyed only by Japanese life and culture, we might wish to remind ourselves of some of the startlingly close parallels that can easily be established with some of the myths within our social fabric.

As a brief example, a derivative myth of the Japanese language is that the language is a vehicle that not only sets apart its speakers and users but also ennobles the users of this special instrument of communication. The ancient poems show that this derivative myth is of equal antiquity with the body of the sociolinguistic concepts around which it is centered, and we have seen the continuation of this theme throughout the literature, down to the present day. For the *Man'yōshū* poets it was the *koto-dama* of the language that "brought blessings to Yamato"; for the modern authors of the sociolinguistic literature this process is still very much alive. For a striking modern parallel, quite apart from the Japanese context, we can consider Theodore White's remarks on the derivative myth that the American office of the President would ennoble anyone who managed to get elected to it.[1] The parallels of this derivative myth of the American presidency with the derivative myth of the *koto-dama* of the Japanese language offer an insight into the two diverse cultures: neither is totally unique or totally original. If a public office can ennoble a man, why cannot a language ennoble and refine the sensitivity of the people who use it? Since derivative myths are even more delicate to investigate and manipulate than the major mythic themes from which they descend, the net conclusion in this area too must be a counsel of extreme caution.

---

[1] Theodore H. White, *Breach of Faith: The Fall of Richard Nixon* (New York: Atheneum, 1975).

97

## Translation and Interpretation

Given the deeply rooted mythic and mystical approach by the Japanese to their language, it is not surprising that volatile and complex situations appear when the language comes in contact with outsiders. Their view of the language necessarily precludes the idea that foreigners will ever fully understand it. Within the assumptions of the Japanese society, one must of necessity be Japanese in order to apprehend the mystical essence of the language. Consequently, when the language is used for dealing with the world beyond Japan, troubles arise. We have examined several areas where the problems caused by this view are particularly acute and significant.

We have seen vivid documentation of the complex matrix of problems that the predominant sociolinguistic approach of the Japanese themselves toward their own language poses for situations in which non-Japanese—particularly Caucasian non-Japanese—learn the Japanese language well enough to use it as a medium of communication. Here the evidence of the sociolinguistic literature suggests tremendously important cautions. The more we learn of the sociolinguistic impact of such multilingual situations within the context of Japanese life and culture, the greater will become our sense of the care required in approaching them. This is part of the overall conclusion of our study: all sociolinguistic situations involving the use of the Japanese language—particularly by non-natives but also by natives—are situations of potentially tremendous sensitivity. What in other cultures would be routine situations of translation and interpretation are in Japan occasions that demand the exercise of extraordinary care and tact. This care and tact can only be exercised on the basis of prior knowledge and at least partial understanding of some of the complex cluster of ideas concerning the nature of the Japanese language that are generally unverbalized commonplaces to the Japanese member of such encounters.

The most practical area in the sociolinguistic field where the conclusion of caution is of particular relevance is that involved with translation and interpretation. It is only when we appreciate the basic proportions of the myth of the Japanese language within Japanese society, and only when we appreciate something of the mystical trappings that surround the sociolinguistic approach of the society toward the language, that we can begin to approach the question of translation and interpretation of Japanese with sufficient seriousness and caution.

It is surely no exaggeration to say that, in any situation involving the translation or interpretation of Japanese into English, the sociolinguistic problems are not solved when the translation or interpretation is completed; they have only begun. A translation from Japanese is, in almost every instance, not a sociolinguistic entity that is able to stand on its own feet; it is not something that is linguistically self-sufficient and able to survive the wrench of isolation involved in separating it from its original text. It is a frail, extremely specialized linguistic organism, and as such it requires special care and attention if it is to survive—particularly if it is to survive to any useful purpose of effective communication, which is, after all, the ostensible goal of all translation and interpretation.

Translation from Japanese for any end—literary, cultural, scientific, political—cannot provide effective communication in isolation from the sociolinguistic approach of the society toward its own language. In Japanese life and culture, translation alone will never provide full communication between Japan and the rest of the world. Translation must always go hand in hand with a full consideration of the background out of which the text being translated has grown. Translation without the assistance of commentary can be worse than no translation at all, because it can be the source of positive misunderstandings and direct crossing of linguistic purposes under the guise of facilitating communication. All the evidence of the sociolinguistic literature points in the direction of this admittedly rather far-reaching conclusion, one that is in essence another recommendation for caution. It is better to have no translation at all than one that attempts to present the content of the original totally without comment or interpretation or reference to the sociolinguistic situation out of which the text in question grew.

With this we have begun to identify an important paradox, something that serves to place the Japanese sociolinguistic situation into sharp contrast with parallel situations elsewhere in the world. Translation and interpretation are, by their very nature, supposed to facilitate interlingual communication. They are supposed to make things easier— and usually they do so. The paradox is that in Japan, and in the case of the Japanese language, this is not necessarily, or even generally, true. Translation and interpretation can make things more difficult; quite as

99

easily as not, they can hinder communication. This is perhaps one of the most important conclusions to be drawn from this survey of the sociolinguistic literature, and it is certainly one of the most important cautions that we must learn to exercise in this field.

This paradox follows directly, of course, from the mysticism with which contemporary Japanese society surrounds itself like a comforting, protective sociolinguistic cocoon, wrapping itself in the many concentric layers of defensive fabric that the myth generates against the intrusions of the outside world. Translation that does not translate and interpretation that does not interpret—such concepts appear at first glance to fly in the face of all common sense. Like everything else involved in the present study, however, they fit into the scheme of things as soon as we consider them within the larger context of the sociolinguistic approach of modern Japanese society to the question of the Japanese language.

The fact that there are paradoxical elements within the Japanese sociolinguistic system should neither surprise nor confuse us now that we perceive the basically mystical orientation of that system itself. Everything about the experience of mysticism is of the nature of a paradox—the ineffable that must nevertheless be described at length; the overwhelming experience of understanding and revelation that is nevertheless incapable of being sustained over any considerable period of time; experiences that carry with them a lasting sense of authority but in which the subject nevertheless describes himself as somehow grasped by some superior power. Thus, it is hardly surprising that we should also locate sociolinguistic paradoxes within the Japanese approach to the Japanese language. The existence of such paradoxes simply confirms our analysis of that sociolinguistic approach as being essentially of the nature of a mystical experience. The paradoxes themselves are classical in nature—that is, they are not truly self-contradictory statements; rather they are assertions that seem to be contradictory and opposed to common sense but that upon careful investigation show themselves to be completely reasonable.

The person who is not a language specialist will surely require whatever consolation the analysis of these paradoxes may provide when he realizes that he is being told, in effect, that the proper utilization of a translation or interpretation from Japanese may very well prove to be quite as difficult a sociolinguistic task as is the work of generating the translation or interpretation in the first place. The user of the translation faces problems that are of equal magnitude with those en-

100

countered by the translator. He must use the translation with the same sensitivity to sociolinguistic concerns and the same attention to the overall sociolinguistic contexts of the culture that the translator has employed. It is well known that translation and interpretation from Japanese into foreign languages, particularly into European languages whose structure differs so greatly from the structure of Japanese, is a task of formidable difficulties. What the present study has revealed is still another layer of difficulty that probably distinguishes Japanese translation from all other translation—the difficulty of using a translation. The difficulties that the sociolinguistic approach of Japanese culture put in the way of such utilization are not insurmountable, but they are very great. It is possible to utilize translation from Japanese, but the successful utilization of such translation is itself dependent upon a set of skills that are, in sum, no less involved and no less precise than those of the translator or interpreter himself. The skills needed involve understanding the sociolinguistic approach of Japanese life and culture toward the language. Without such understanding, translation may turn out to be worse than total ignorance of Japanese texts, and interpretation may lead only to misinterpretation.

Again, the overall conclusion of the present study may be summed up under the rubric of caution. We have surely seen enough here of the sociolinguistic fallout from the phenomenology of mysticism with which Japanese culture has surrounded its approach to the language so that we can begin to understand why nothing involving the language as it operates vis-à-vis the society can be approached simply. Caution—implying constant attention, and the greatest possible sensitivity, to the sociolinguistic concerns of modern Japan—is the conclusion to be drawn from what we have here been able to learn from the literature. The translator's work may be over when the translation is finished, but the work of true translation—the work of genuine interpretation, in the sense of valid cross-cultural communication—has at that point just begun. To continue it, and ideally to complete it, represents another, and an equally involved, task. This is a task that can only be approached with as much cultural caution and sociolinguistic sensitivity as we can possibly summon.

Furthermore, this sensitivity must be exercised over a broad spectrum of issues, only a few of which have been discussed here. But these issues are problems of a quality and of a nature that may very well strike the observer who is unfamiliar with Japanese life and culture as unusual in the extreme. The work of the specialist is to identify these problems for the nonspecialist and thus gradually to make it possible for him to operate with increasing skill in this difficult and demanding field. Such identification of problems, together with a preliminary attempt at their description and analysis, has been the principal goal of this study.

# Bibliography

Chamberlain, Basil Hall. *Things Japanese, being notes on various subjects connected with Japan, for the use of travelers and others.* 1904. Reprint (under title *Japanese Things*). Tokyo: Charles E. Tuttle Co., 1974.

Goldstein, Bernice, and Tamura, Kyoko. *Japan and America: A Comparative Study in Language and Culture.* Tokyo: Charles E. Tuttle Co., 1975.

Hall, Ivan Parker. *Mori Arinori.* Cambridge: Harvard University Press, 1973.

Hattori Shirō. *Nihongo no keitō* [The genetic relationships of the Japanese language]. Tokyo: Iwanami Shoten, 1957.

Ikeda Mayako. *Nihongo saihakken, ishitsu no ninshiki* [The rediscovery of Japanese: my realization of its different nature] Sanseidō shinsho [Sanseidō new library] no. 117. Tokyo: Sanseidō, 1973.

————. *Soto kara mita Nihongo, Washinton daigaku no 'Nihongo kurasu'* [Japanese seen from the outside: the University of Washington's Japanese language classes]. Sanseidō shinsho [Sanseidō new library] no. 29. Tokyo: Sanseidō, 1968.

Itasaka Gen. *Nihongo yokochō* [Back streets of the Japanese language]. Tokyo: Shibundō, 1975.

Itō Haku. "Man'yōjin to *kotodama*" [People of the *Man'yō* period and the "soul of language"]. In *Man'yōshū kōza* [Lectures on the *Man'yōshū*], edited by Hisamatsu Sen'ichi. Vol. 3, *Gengo to hyōgen* [Language and expression]. Tokyo: Yūseidō, 1973.

James, William. *The Varieties of Religious Experience: A Study in Human Nature.* With a new introduction by Reinhold Niebuhr. New York: Macmillan Co., 1961.

Kamei Takashi. *Chinese Borrowings in Prehistoric Japanese.* Tokyo: Shibundō, 1954.

Kindaichi Haruhiko. *Nihongo* [The Japanese language]. Iwanami shinsho [Iwanami new library], no. 265. Tokyo: Iwanami Shoten, 1957.

Kokugo gakkai [Japanese language association]. *Kokugogaku jiten* [Dictionary of Japanese language studies]. 17th ed. rev. Tokyo: Tōkyōdō, 1969.

Ledyard, Gari. "Galloping Along with the Horseriders: Looking for the Founders of Japan." *Journal of Japanese Studies*. Vol. 1 (1975), pp. 217-254.

Miller, Roy Andrew. *Bernard Bloch on Japanese*. New Haven: Yale University Press, 1969.

―――. *'The Footprints of the Buddha,'* an *Eighth-century Old Japanese Poetic Sequence*. American Oriental Series, vol. 58. New Haven: American Oriental Society, 1975.

―――. *Japanese and the Other Altaic Languages*. Chicago: University of Chicago Press, 1971.

―――. *The Japanese Language*. Chicago: University of Chicago Press, 1967.

―――. "Levels of Speech (*keigo*) and the Japanese Linguistic Response to Modernization." In *Tradition and Modernization in Japanese Culture*, edited by Donald H. Shively. Princeton: Princeton University Press, 1971.

―――. "The Origins of Japanese." *Monumenta Nipponica*. Vol. 29 (1974), pp. 93-102.

Miura Tsutomu. *Nihongo wa dō yu gengo ka?* [What kind of language is Japanese?] Tokyo: Kisetsusha, 1971.

Miyoshi, Masao. *Accomplices of Silence: The Modern Japanese Novel*. Berkeley: University of California Press, 1974.

Nippon Gakujutsu Shinkokai. *The Manyōshū, The Nippon Gakujutsu Shinkōkai Translation of One Thousand Poems*. Tokyo: Iwanami Shoten, 1940. Reprint. New York: Columbia University Press, 1965.

Ohno, Susumu. *The Origin of the Japanese Language*. Tokyo: Kokusai Bunka Shinkōkai, 1970. Japanese original in Ōno 1957.

Omodaka Hisakata; Asami Tetsu; Ikegami Teizō; Ide Itaru; Itō Hiroshi; Kawabata Yoshiaki; Kinoshita Masatoshi; Kojima Noriyuki; Sakakura Atsuyoshi; Satake Akihiro; Nishimiya Kazutami; and Hashimoto Shirō, eds. *Jidaibetsu kokugo daijiten, Jōdaihen* [Unabridged dictionary of the Japanese language by periods: Old Japanese]. Tokyo: Sanseidō, 1967.

Ōno Susumu. *Man'yōshu* [Anthology of a myriad leaves]. Nihon koten bungaku taikei [Corpus of Japanese classical literature], vol. 5. Tokyo: Iwanami Shoten, 1959.

―――. *Nihongo no kigen* [The origin of the Japanese language]. Iwanami shinsho [Iwanami new library], no. 289. Tokyo: Iwanami Shoten, 1957. English translation in Ohno 1970.

―――. *Nihongo wo sakanoboru* [Tracing back the history of Japanese]. Iwanami shinsho [Iwanami new library], no. 911. Tokyo: Iwanami Shoten, 1974.

Ōno Susumu, Satake Akihiro, and Maeda Kingorō. *Iwanami kogo jiten* [The Iwanami dictionary of earlier forms of Japanese]. Tokyo: Iwanami Shoten, 1974.

Suzuki Takao. *Kotoba to shakai* [Language and society]. Tokyo: Chūō Kōronsha, 1975.

————. *Tozasareta gengo—Nihongo no sekai* [The world of Japanese—a locked-up language]. Tokyo: Shinchōsha, 1975.

Terry, Charles. "Sakuma Shōzan and his Seiken-roku." Master's thesis, Columbia University, 1951.

Watanabe, Shoichi. "On the Japanese language." *Japan Echo*. Vol. 1 (Winter 1974), pp. 9-20.